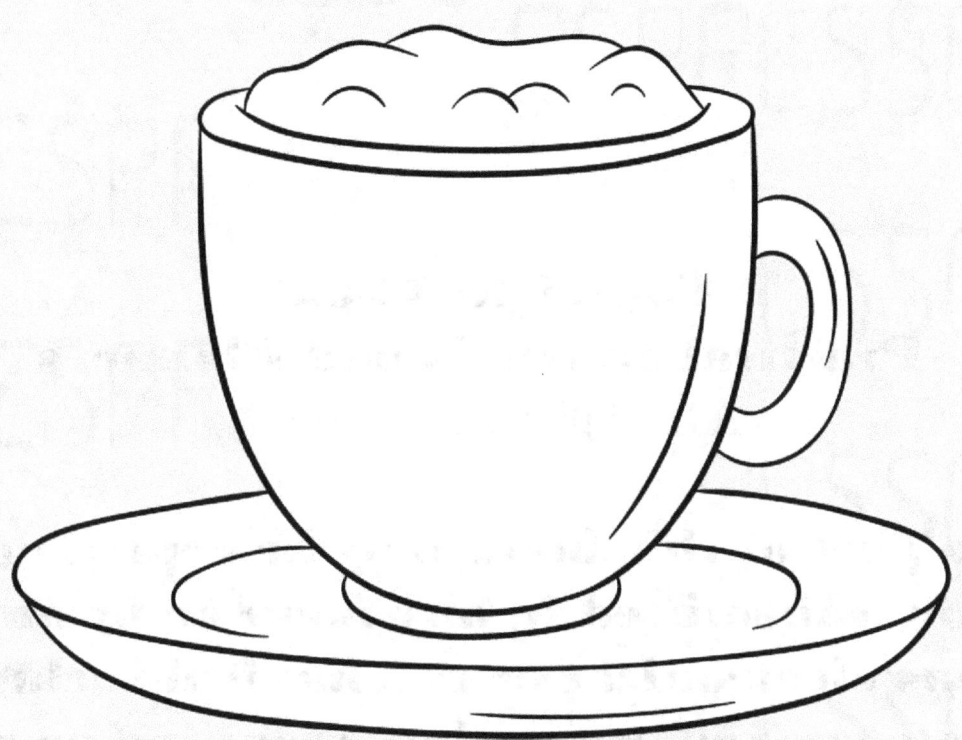

This Book Belongs To:

_____

_____

Copyright ©2020
Practical Journals and Planners
All rights reserved.

No part of this book may be reproduced or transmitted in any form or by any means electronical or mechanical including photocopying, recording, scanning or any other information storage retrieval system without permission from the Publisher.

www.PracticalJournalsandPlanners.com

Cut out this page, following the line, and place the page under your drawing to color it safely.

It is best practice to use crayons, colored pencils, and gel/glitter pens for coloring this book instead of using markers or watercolor paints.

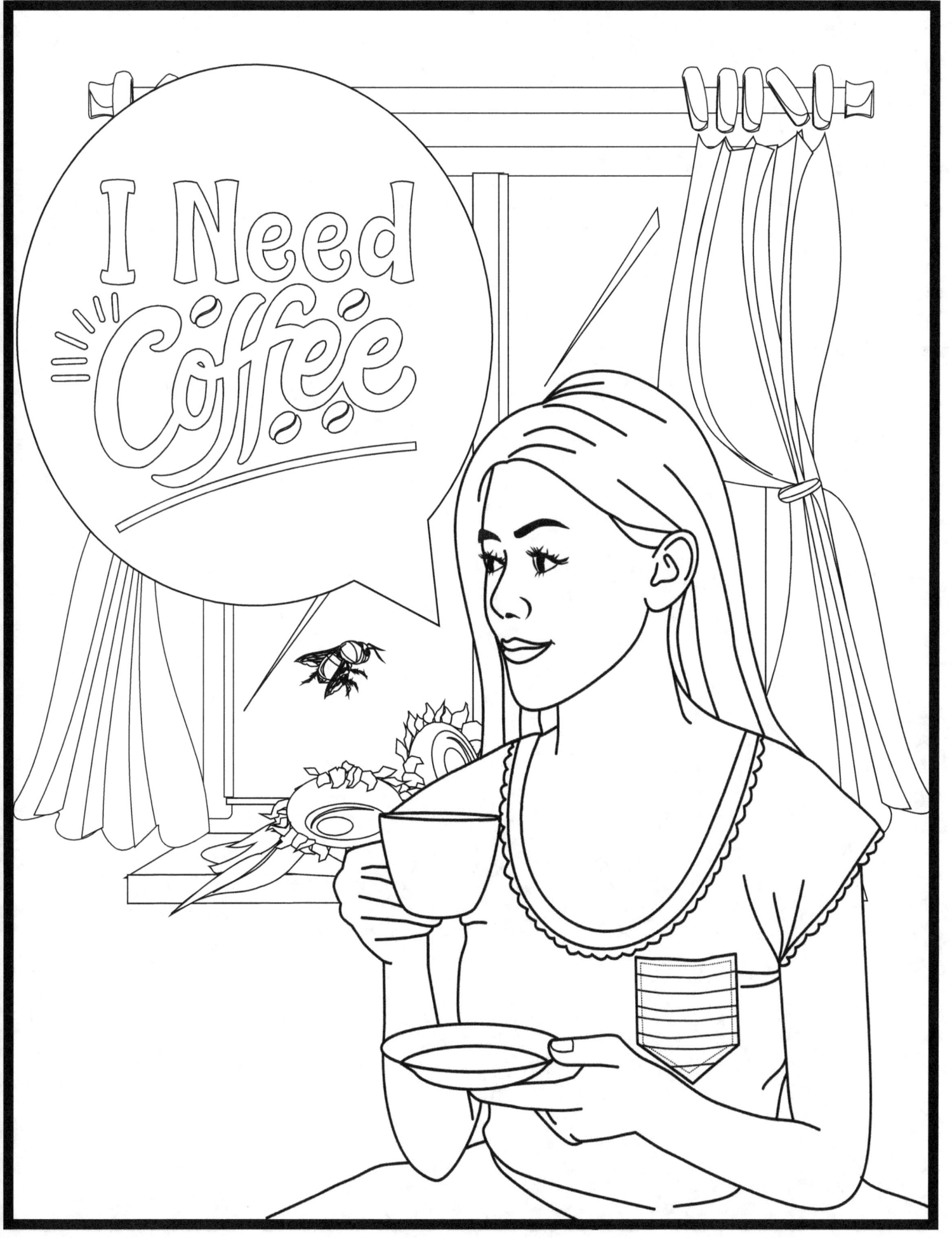

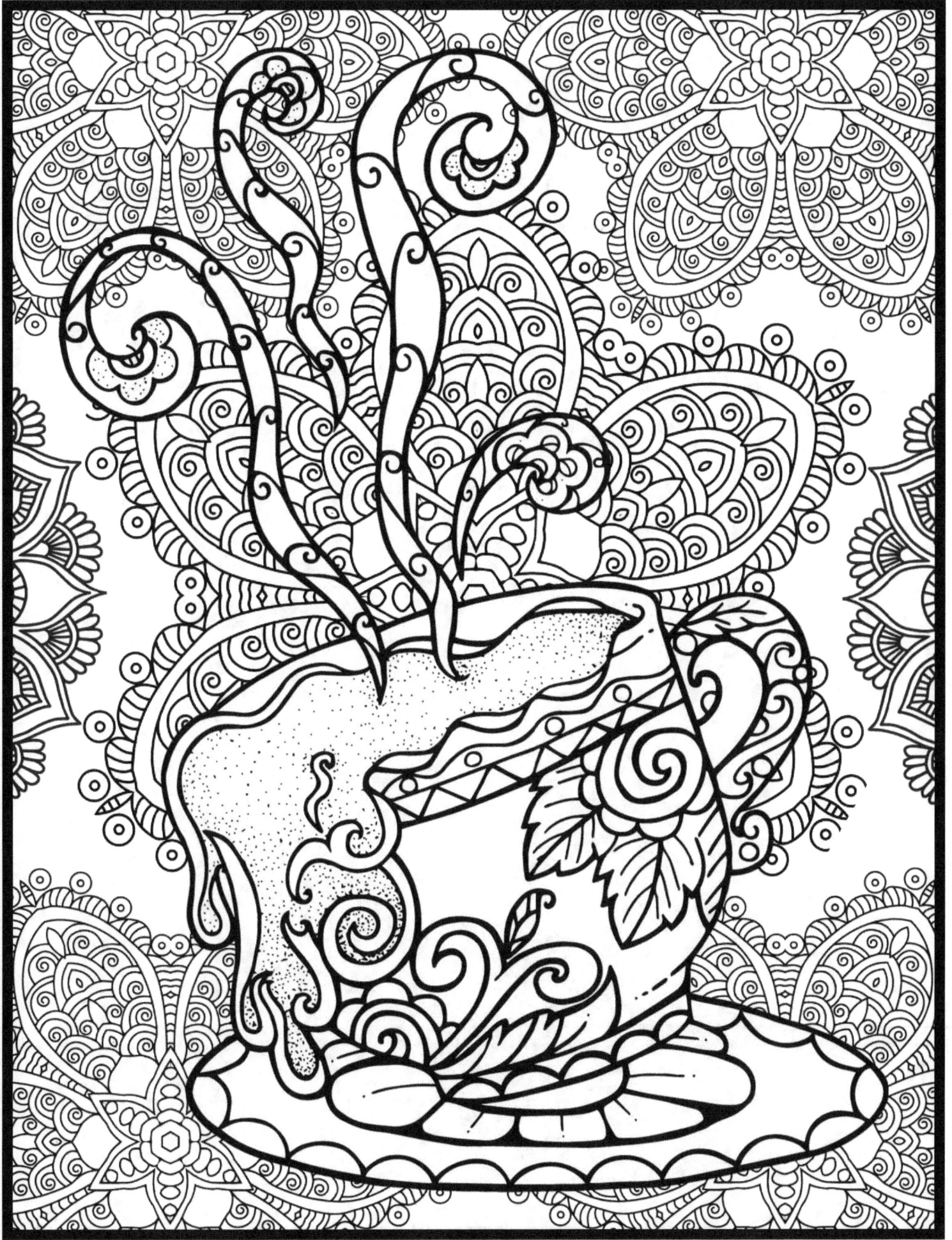

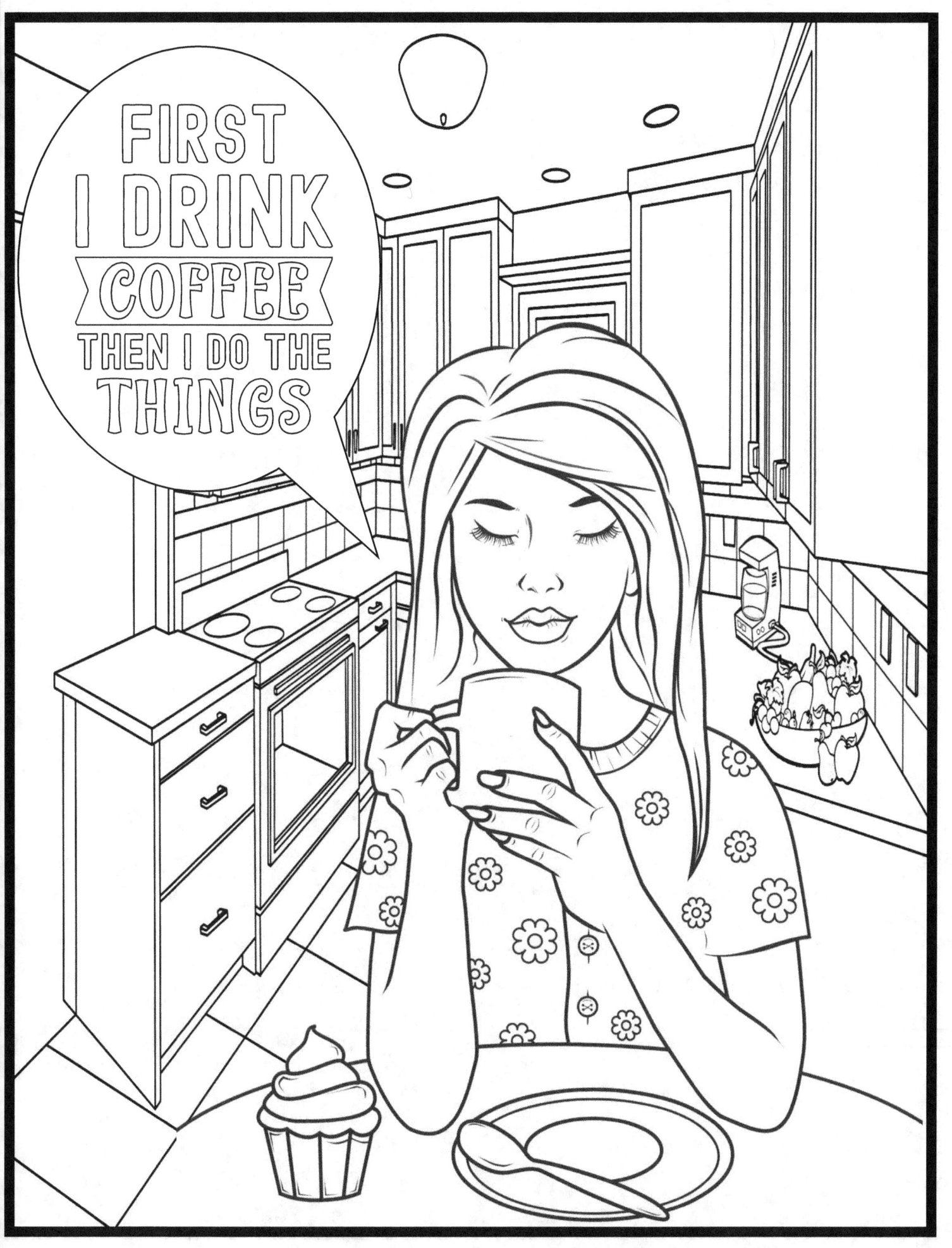

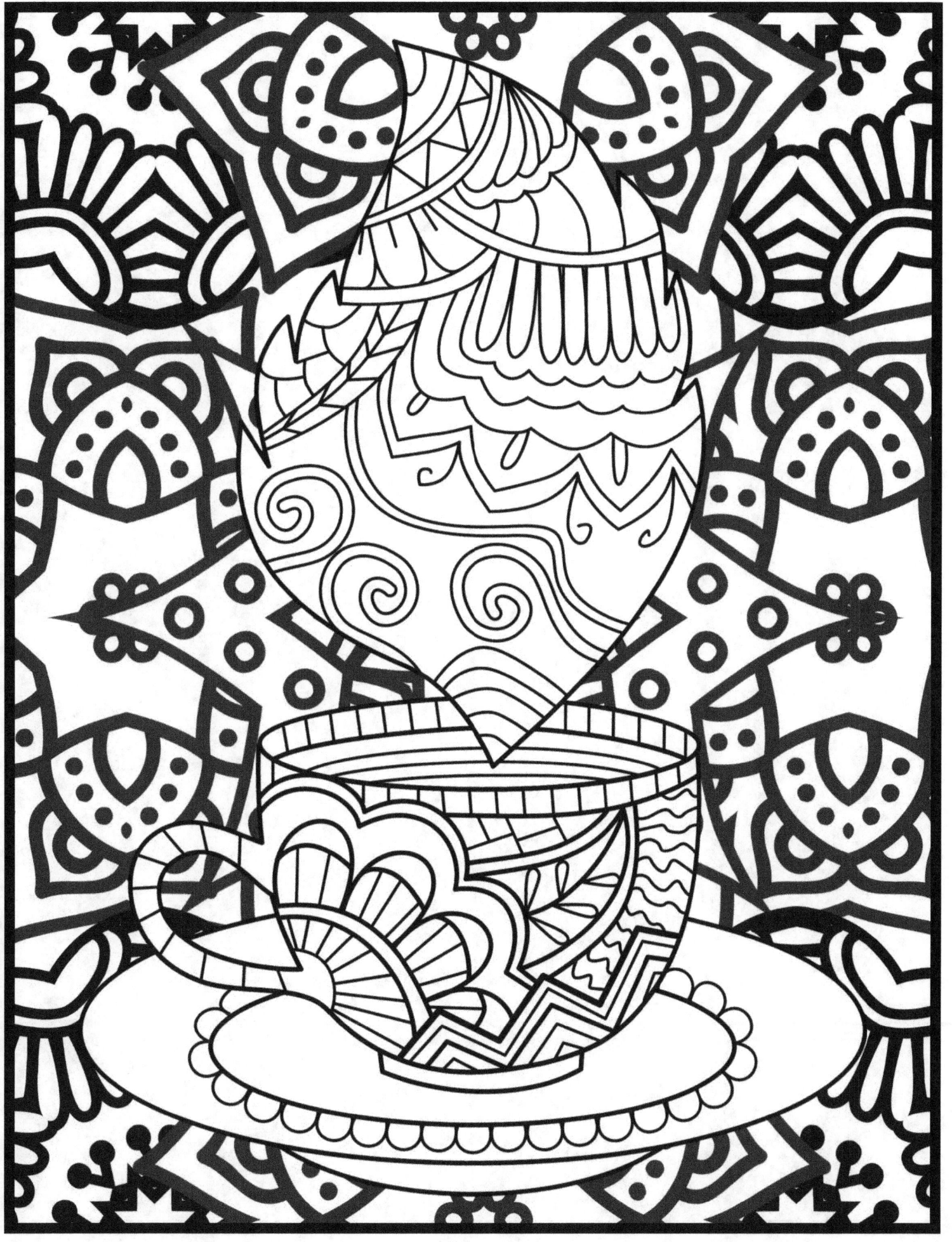

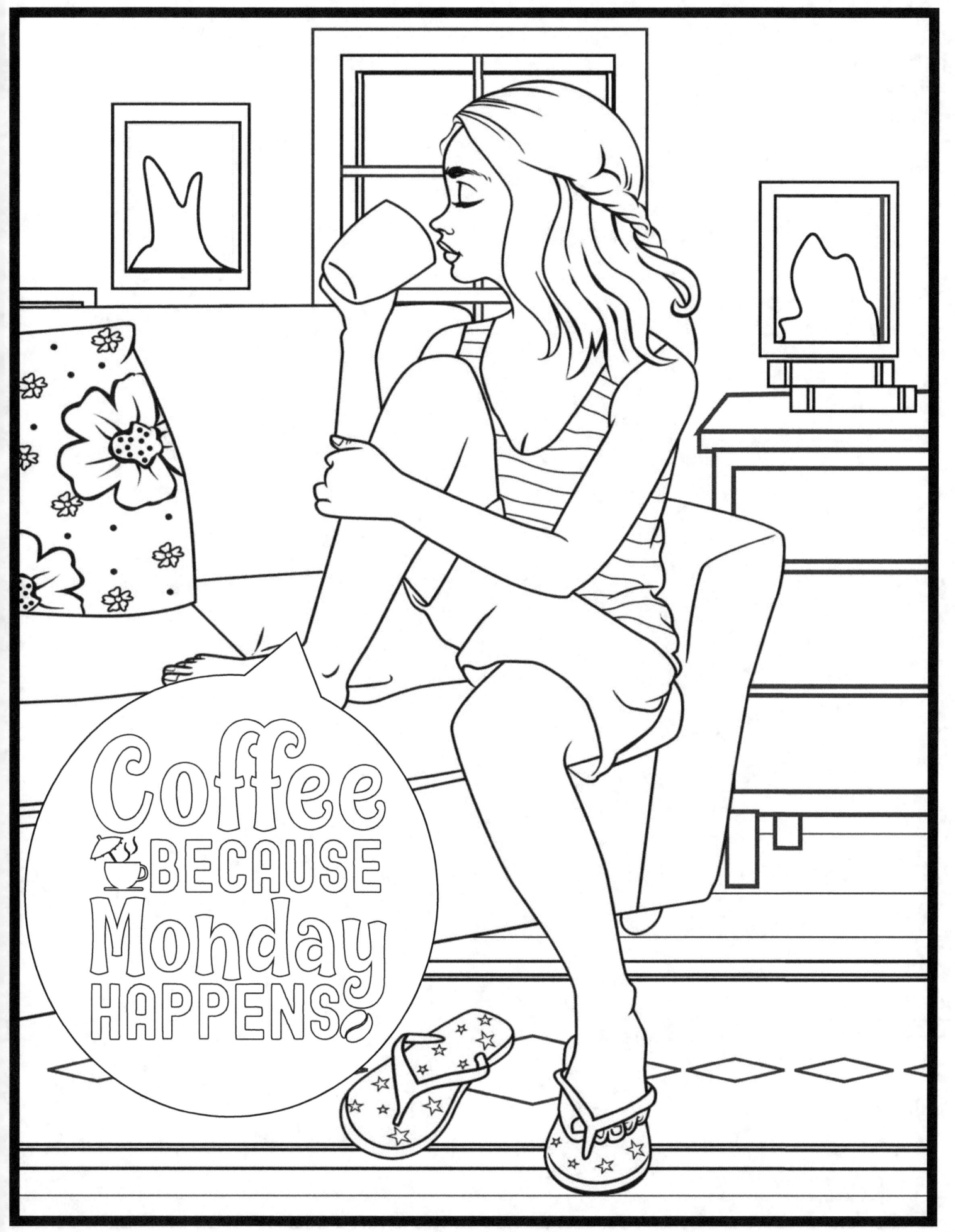

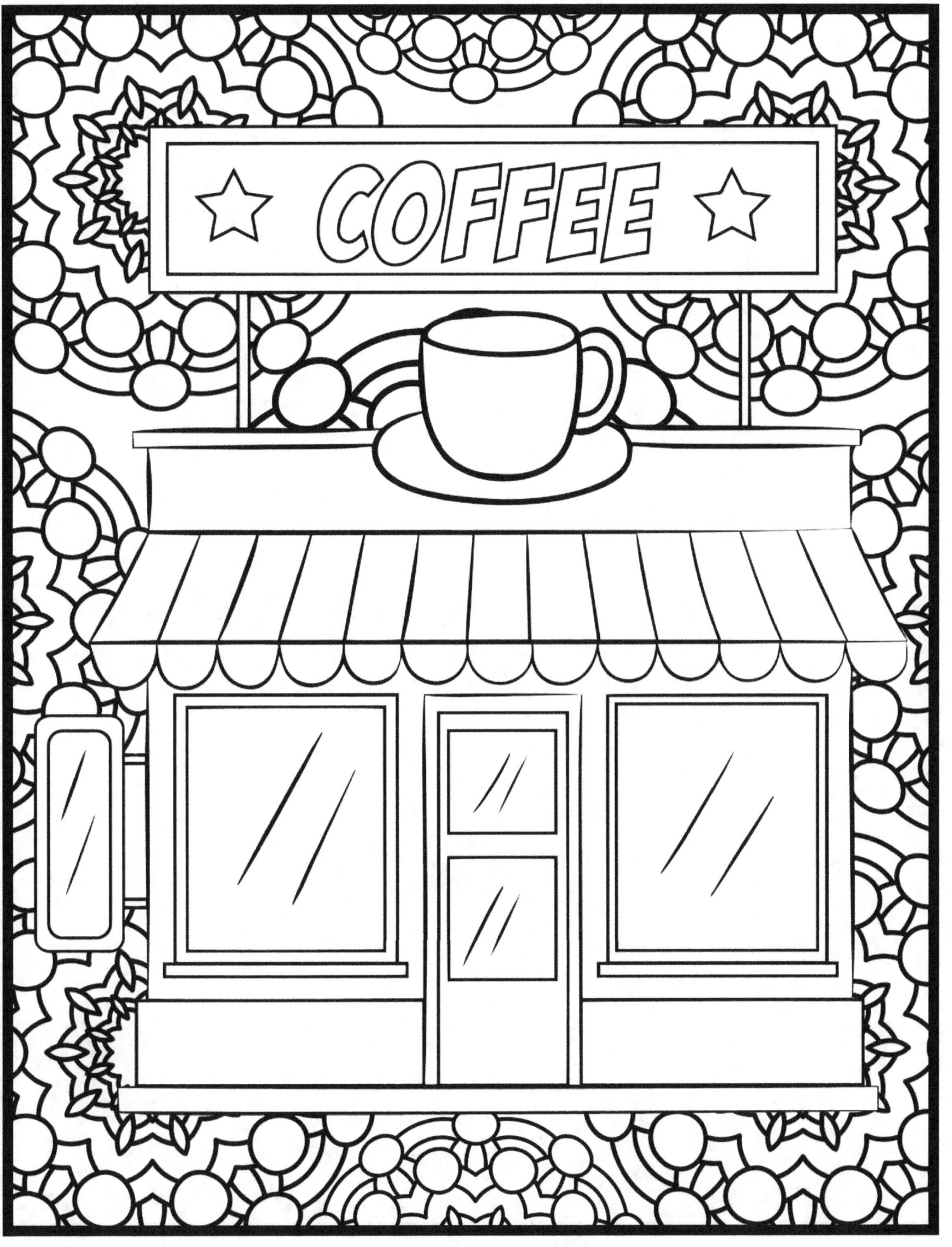

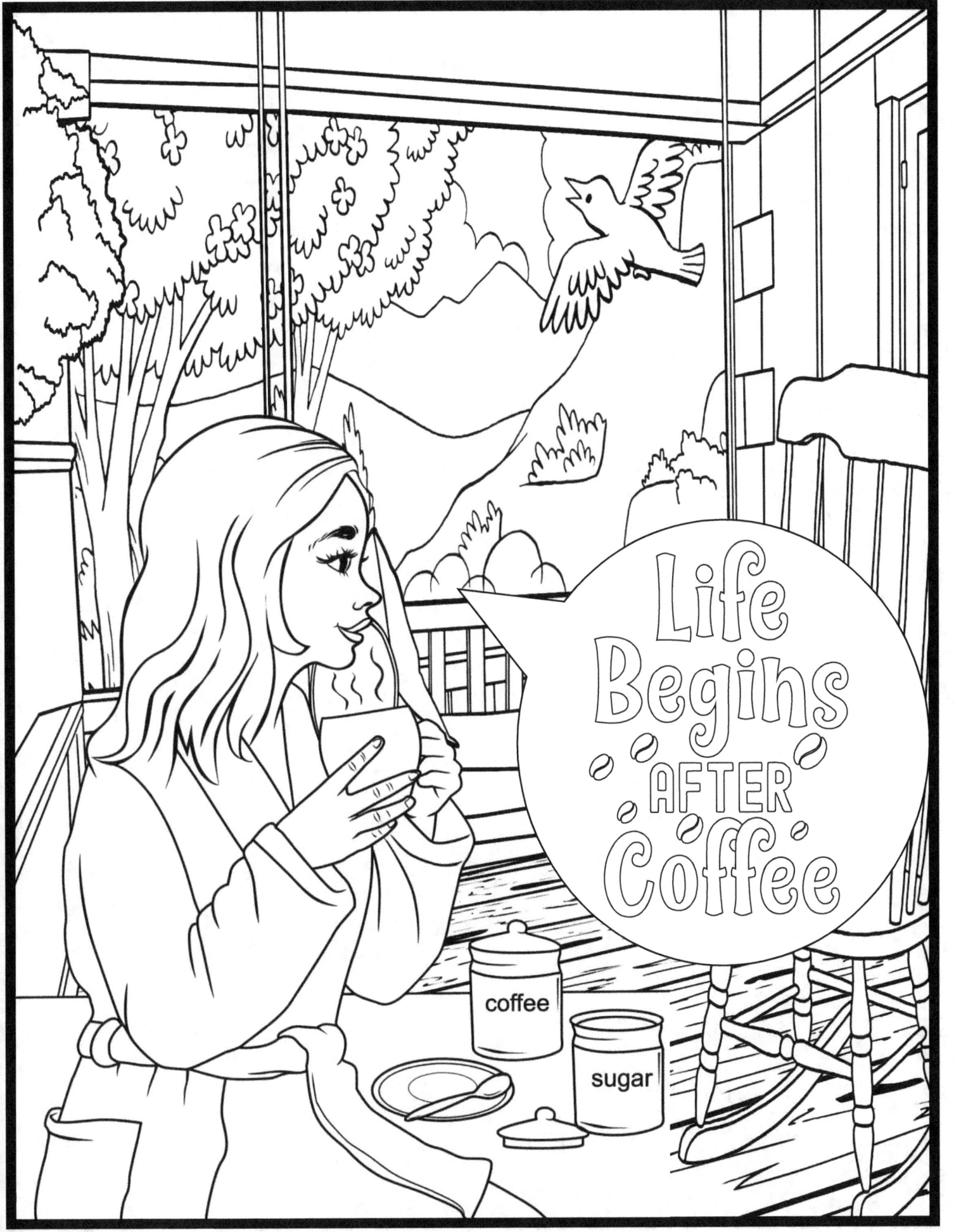

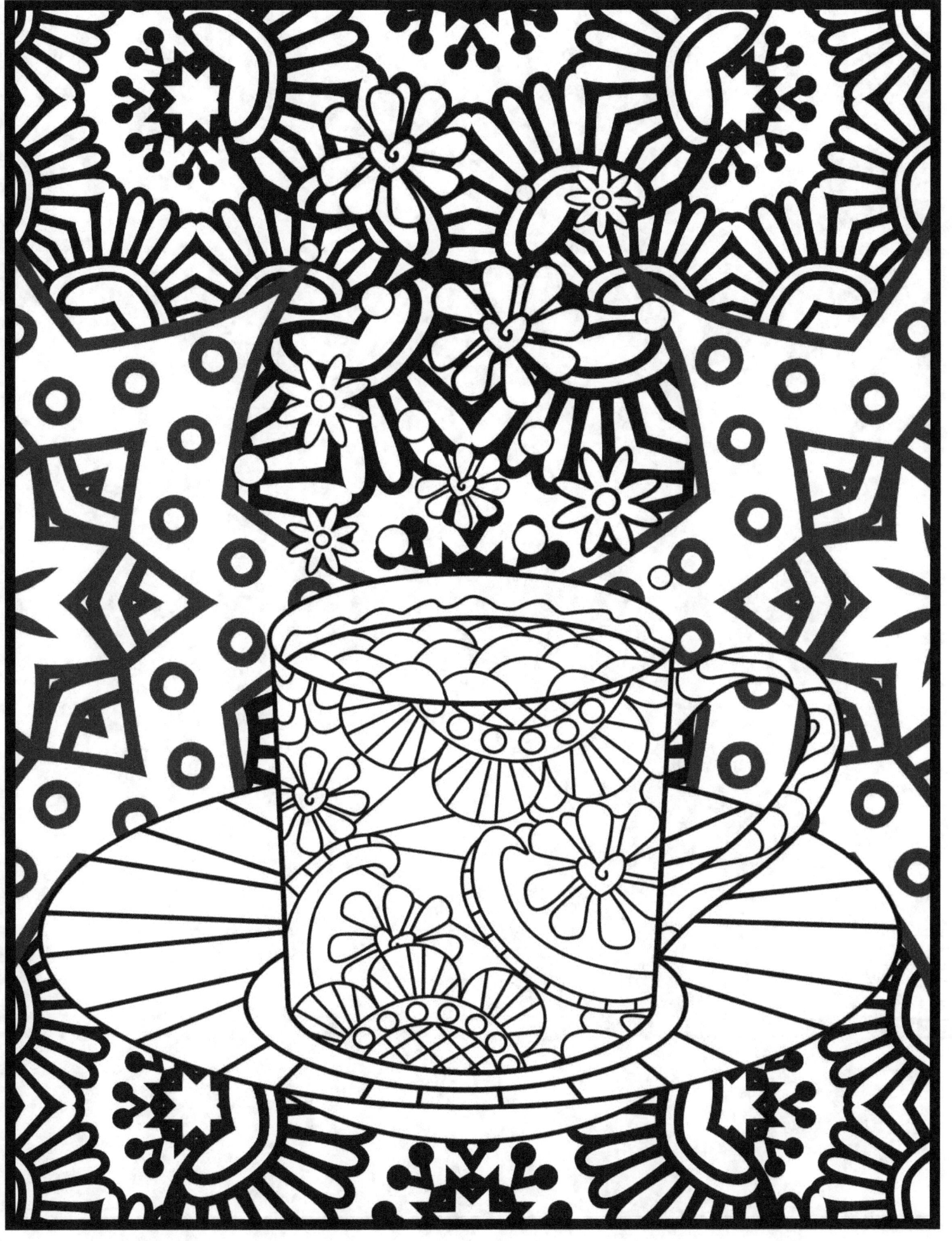

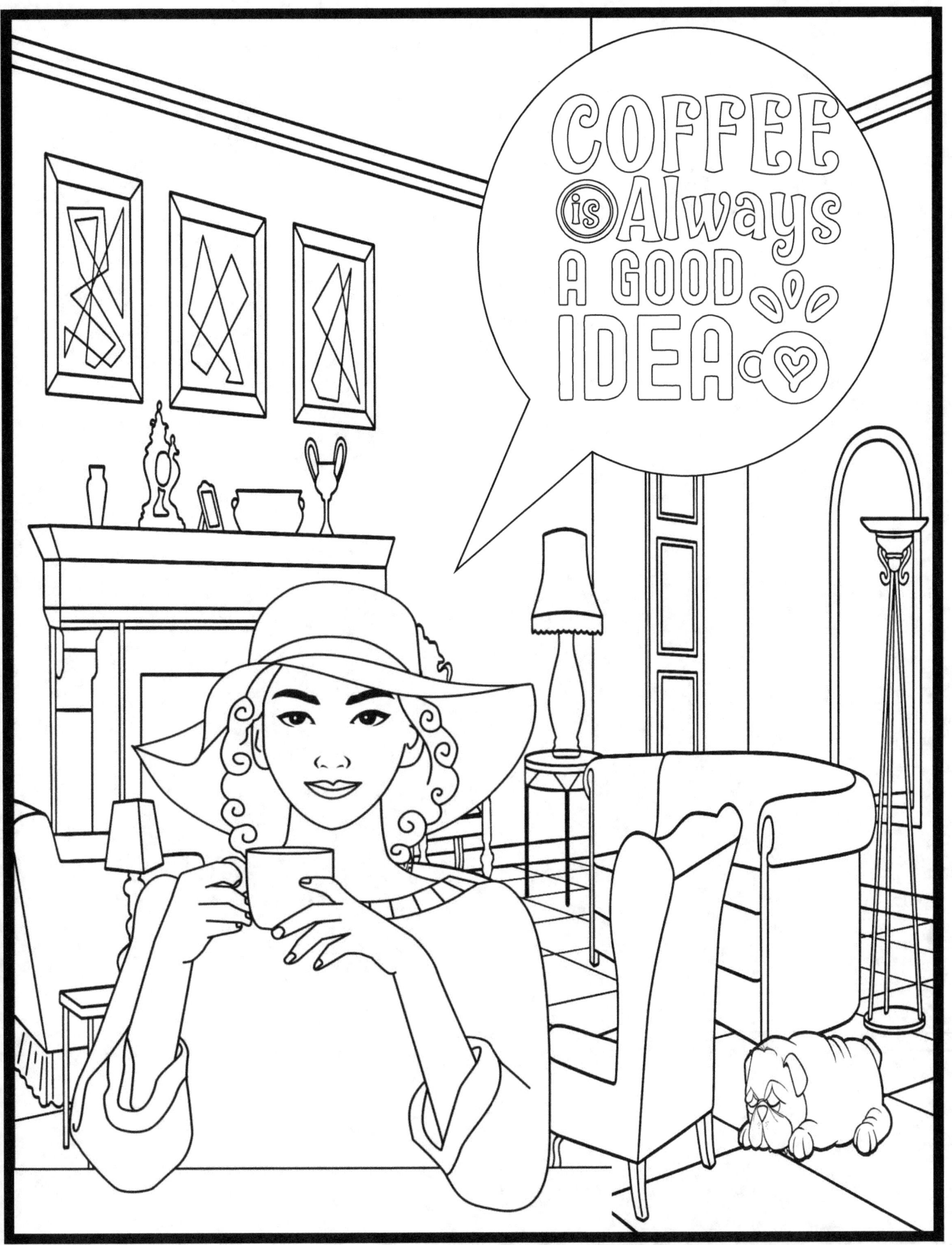

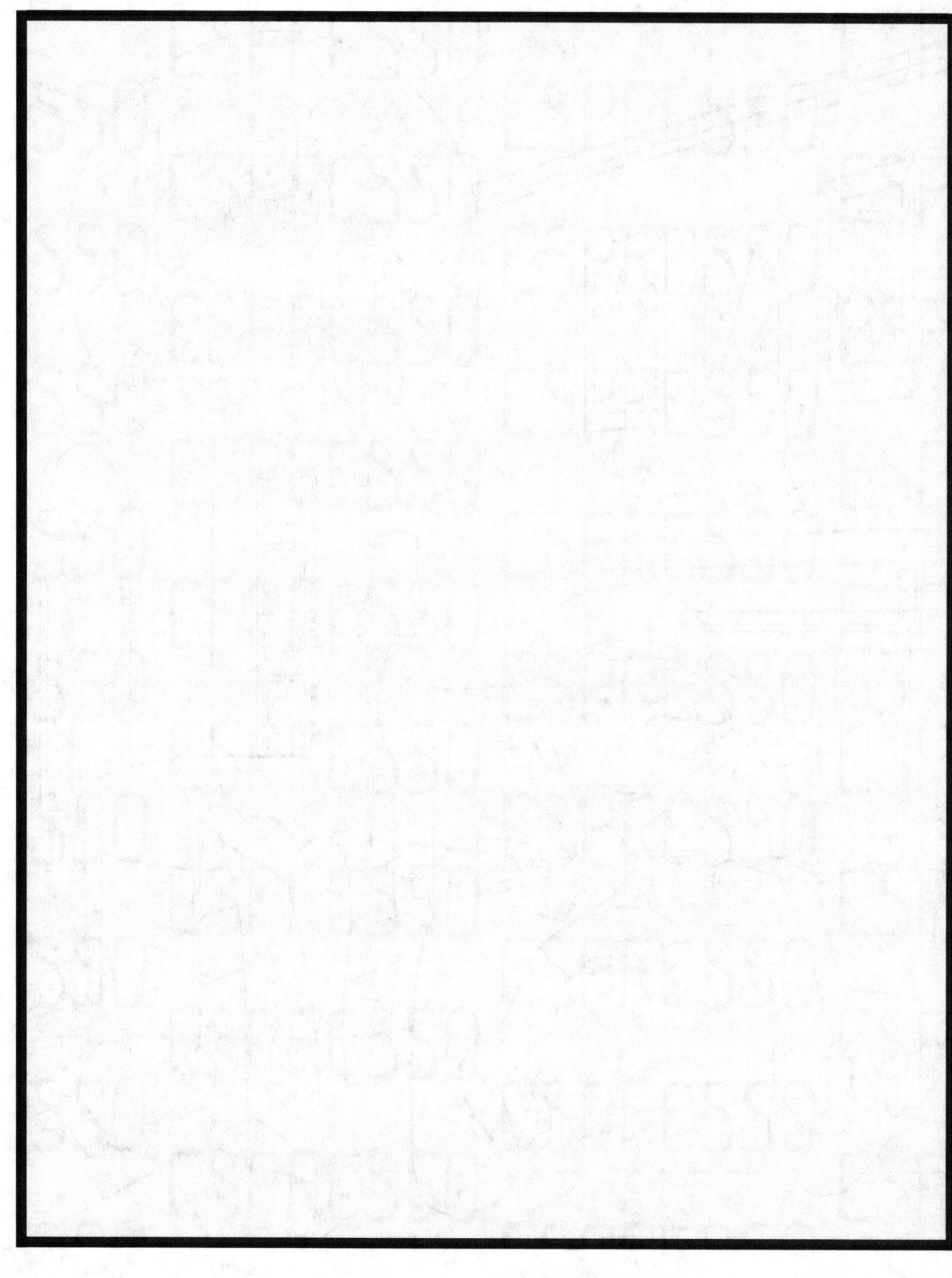

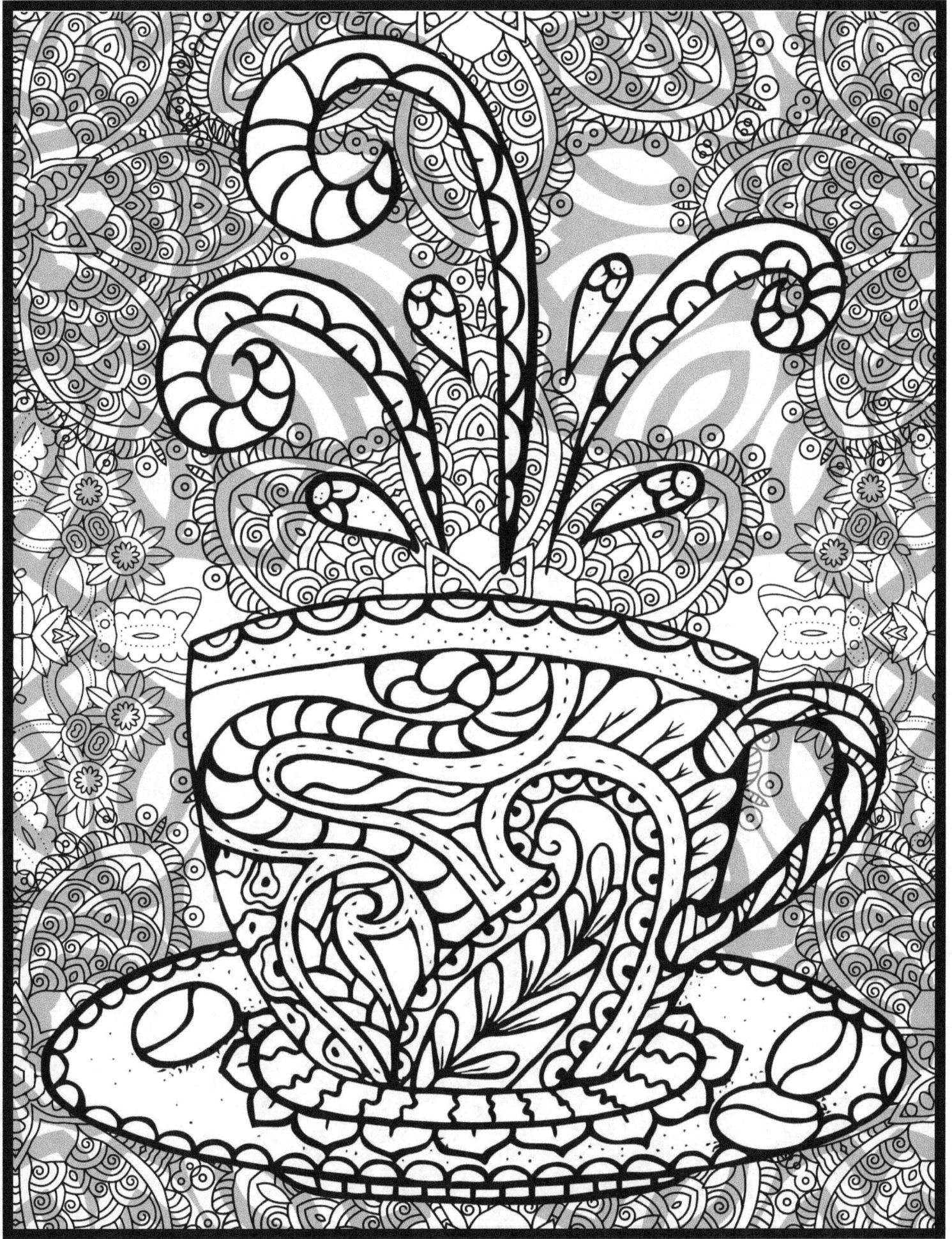

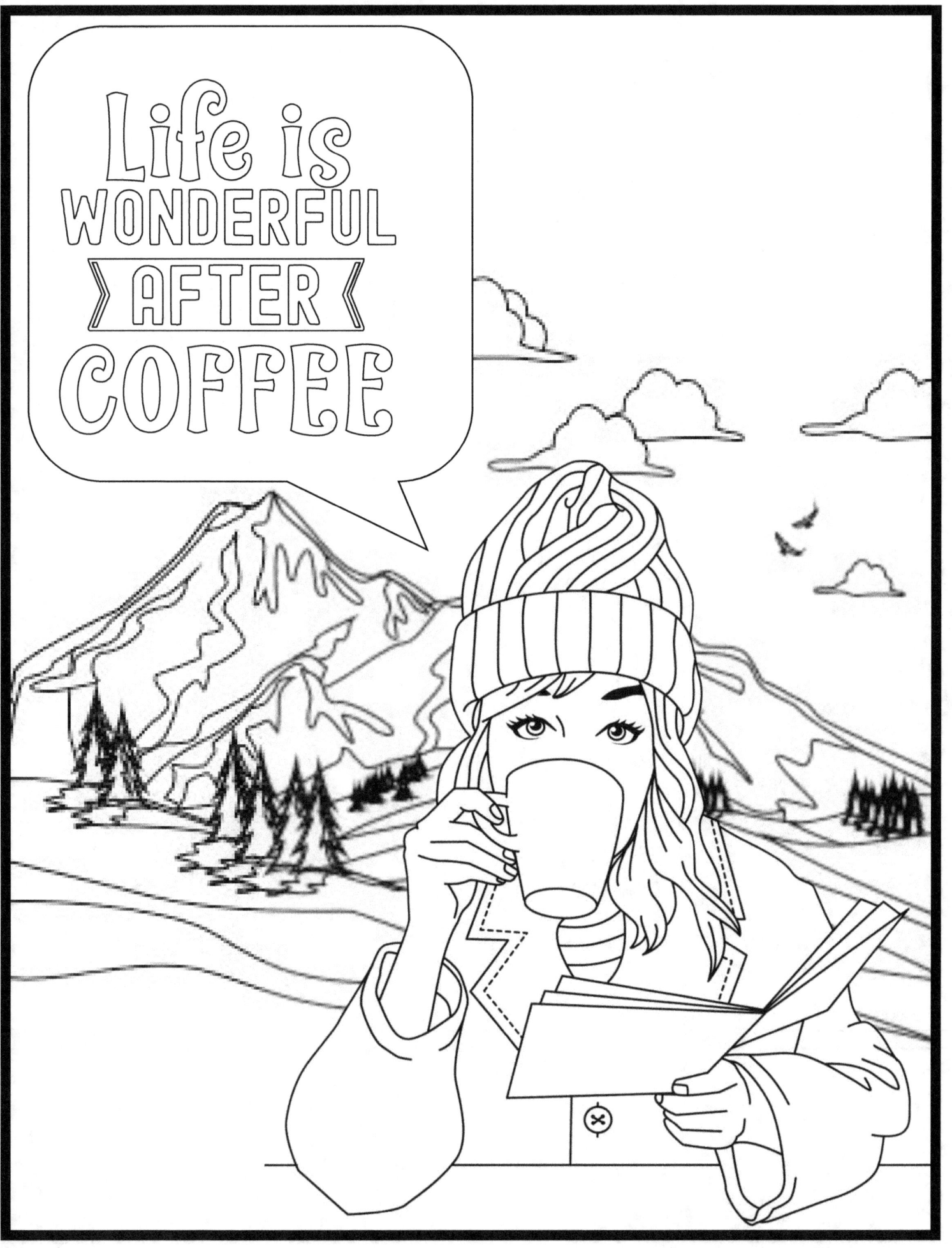

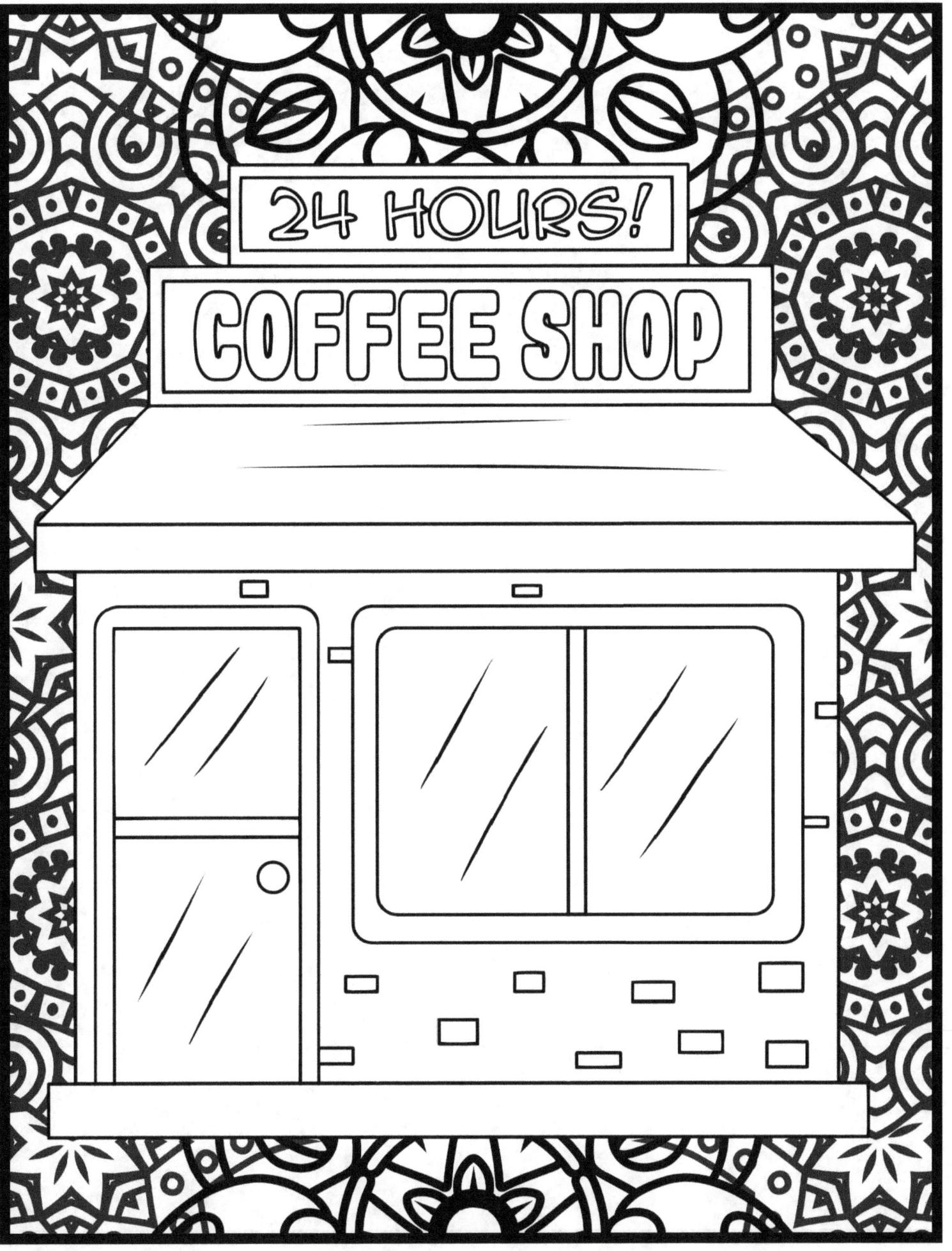

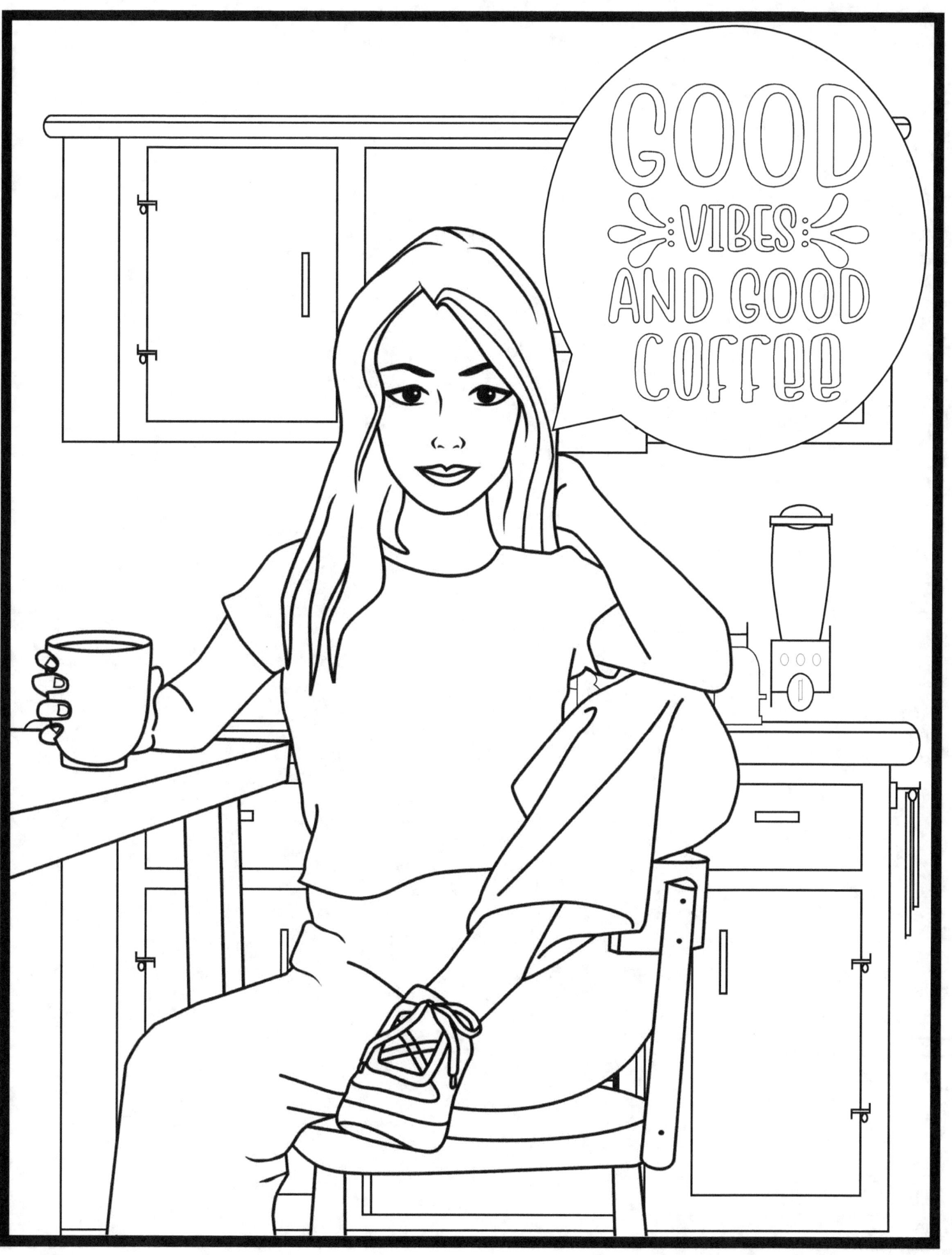

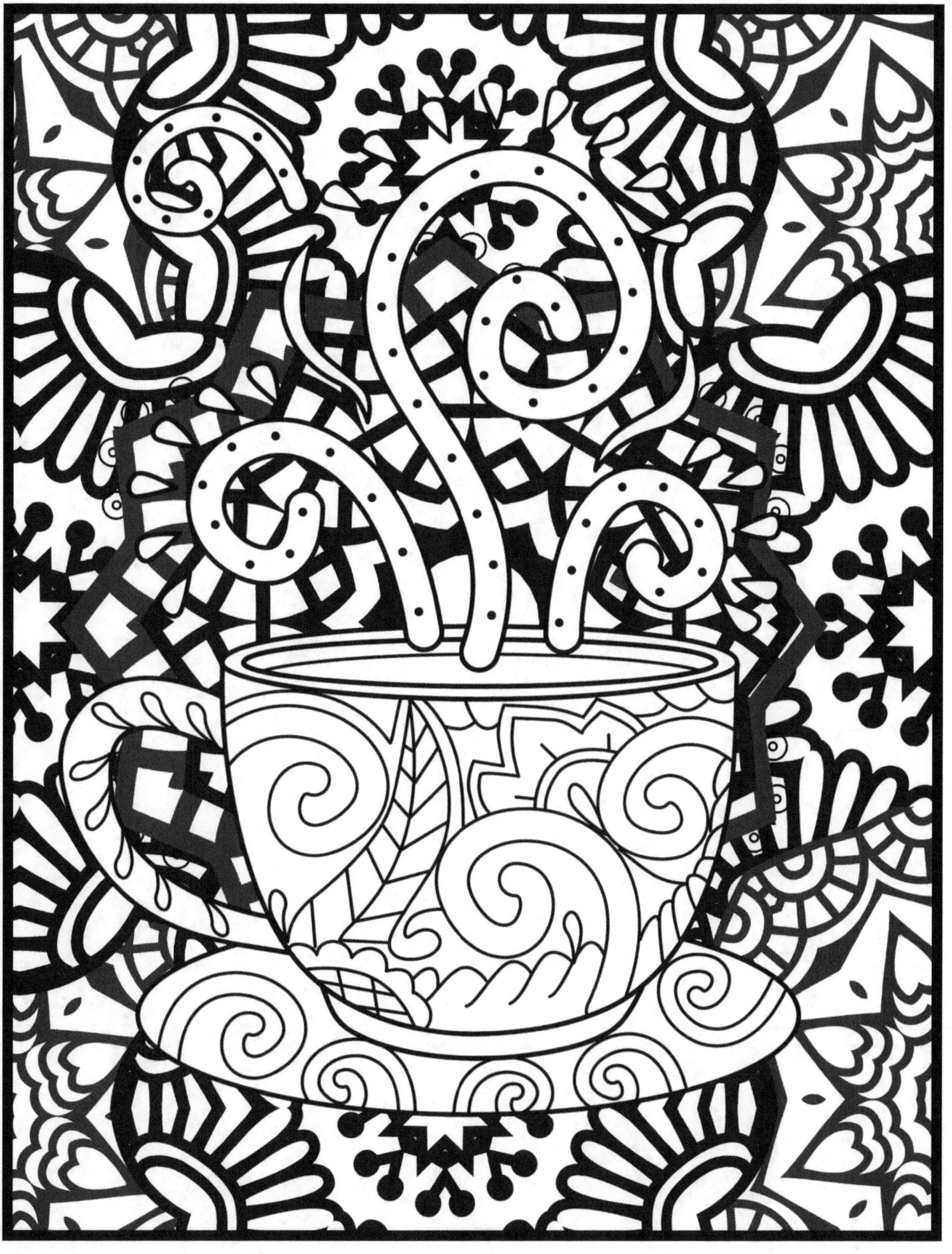

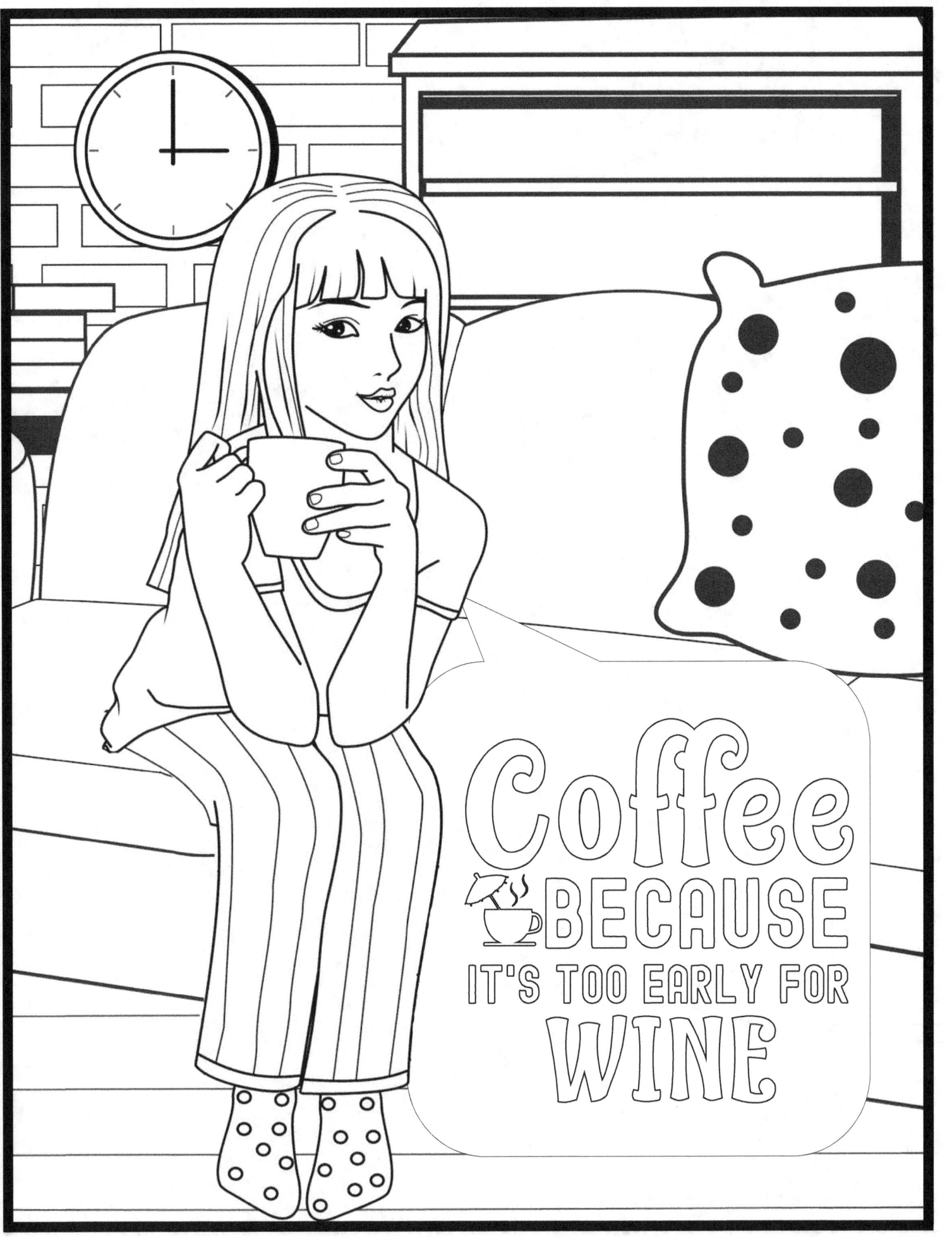

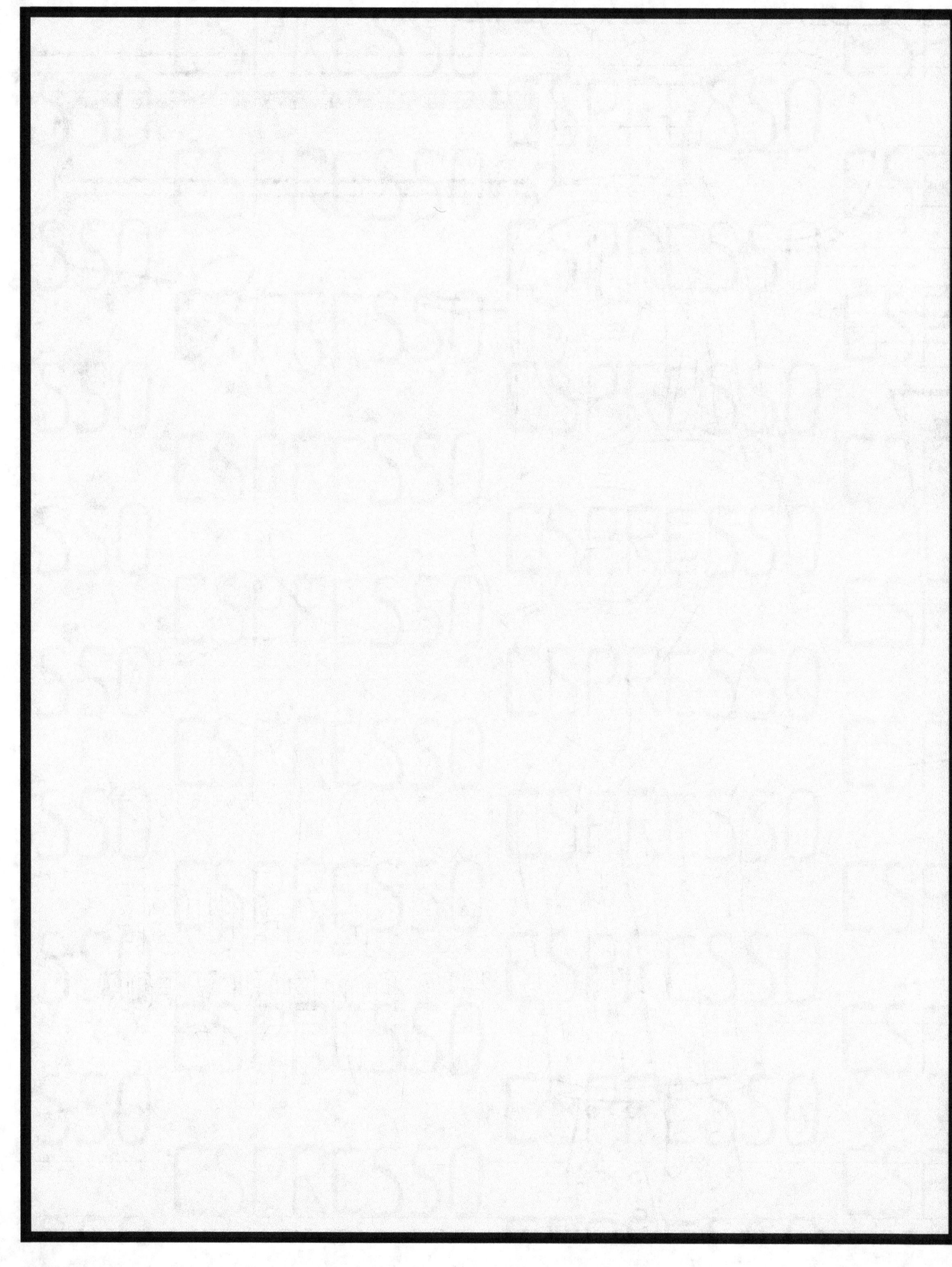

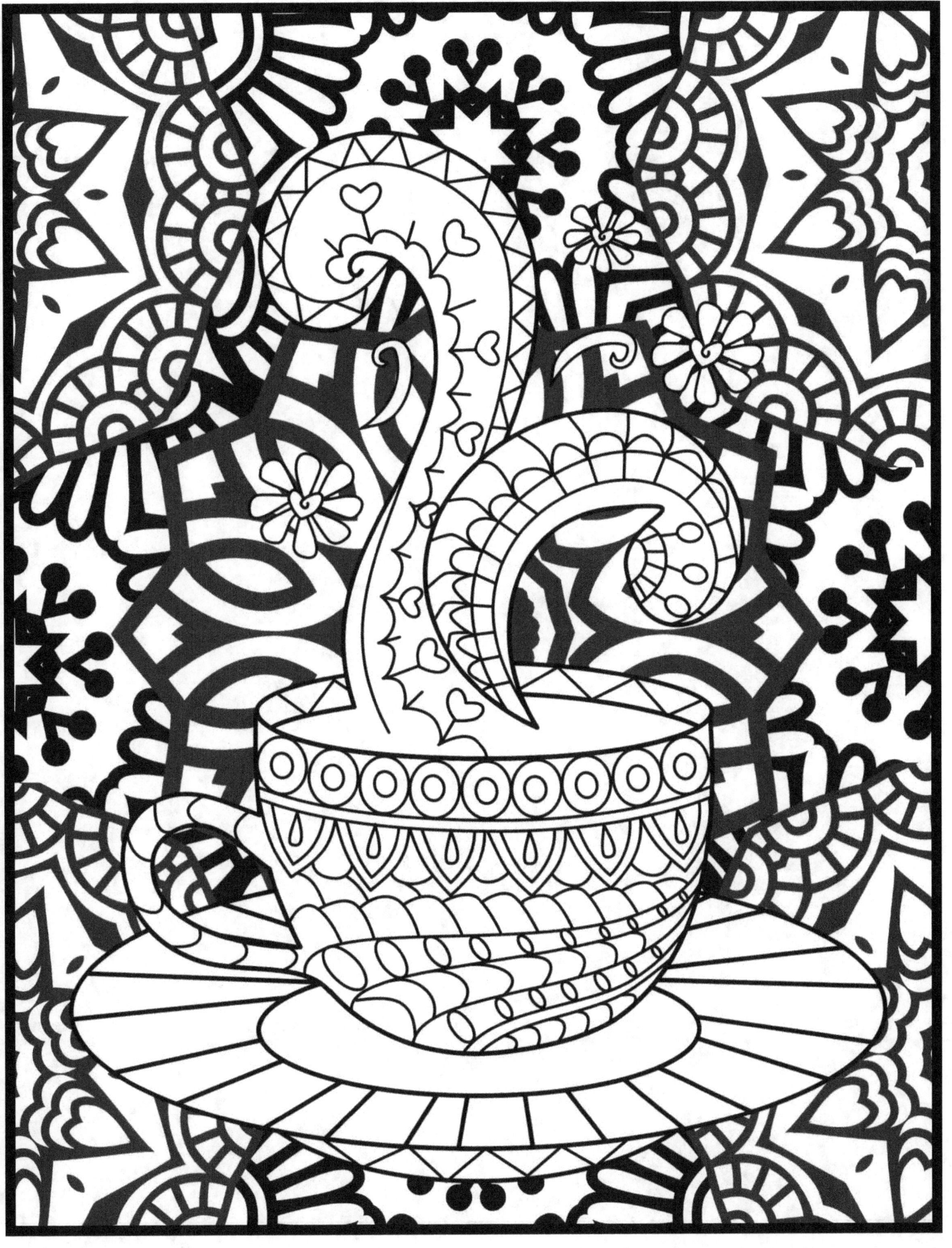

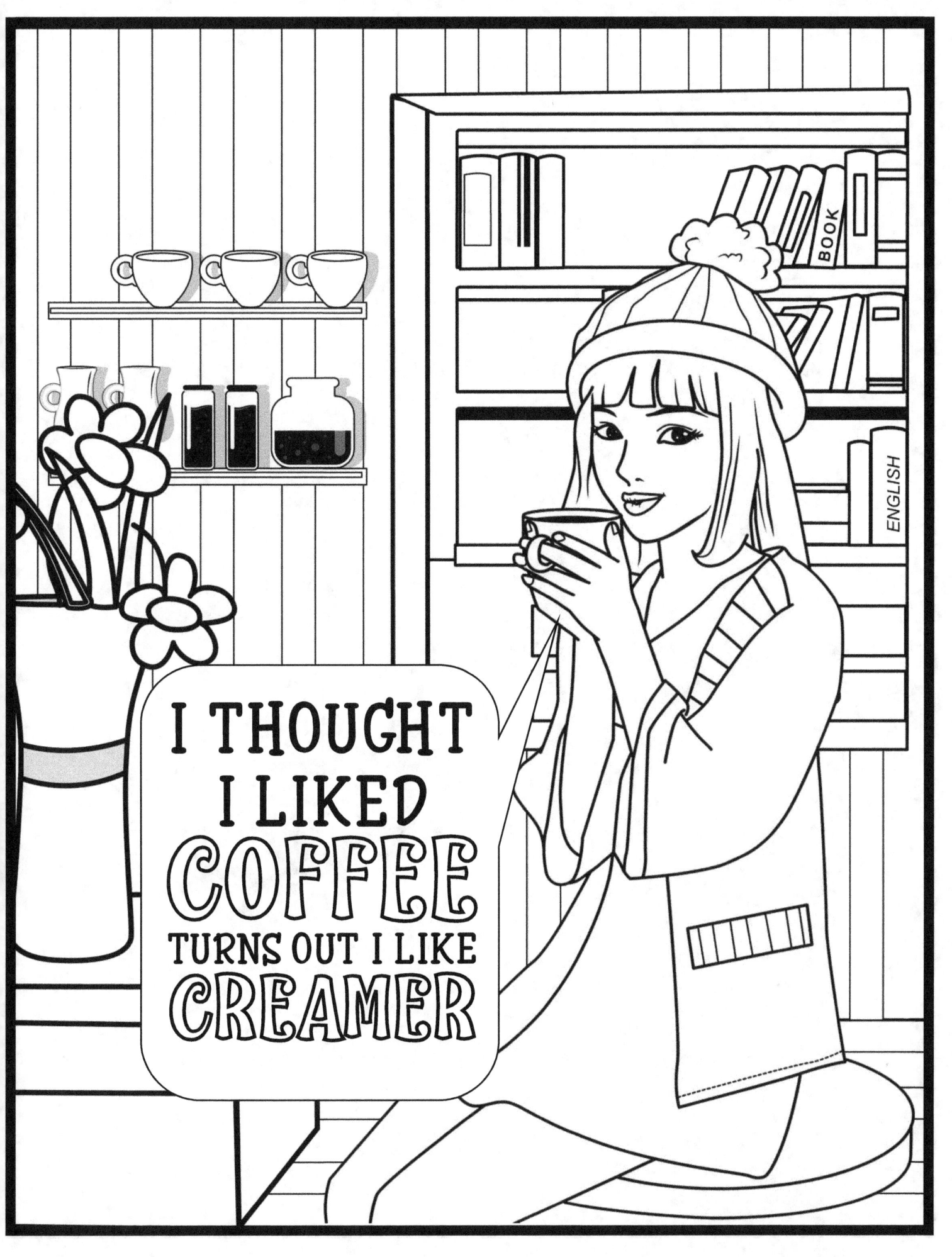

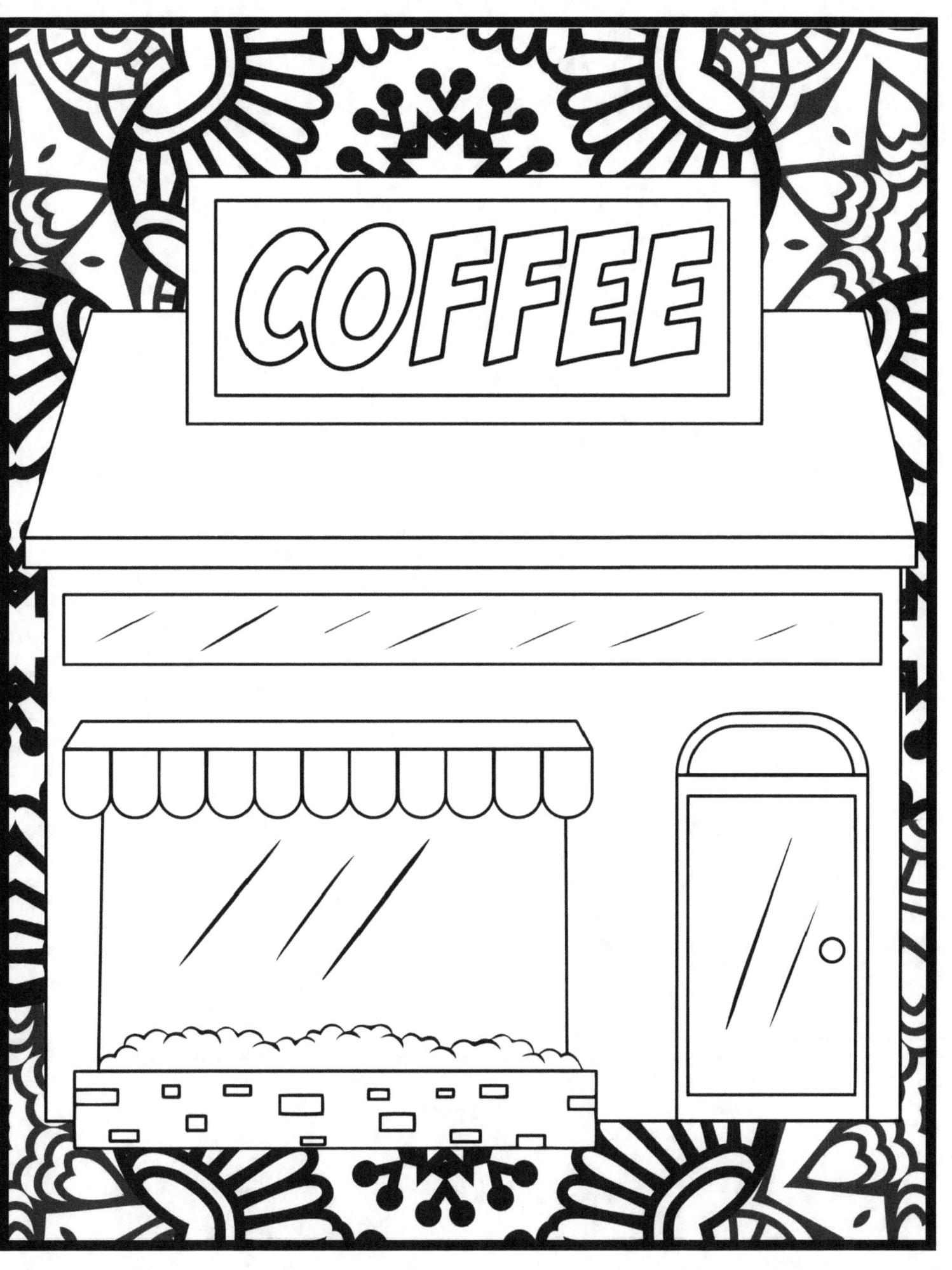

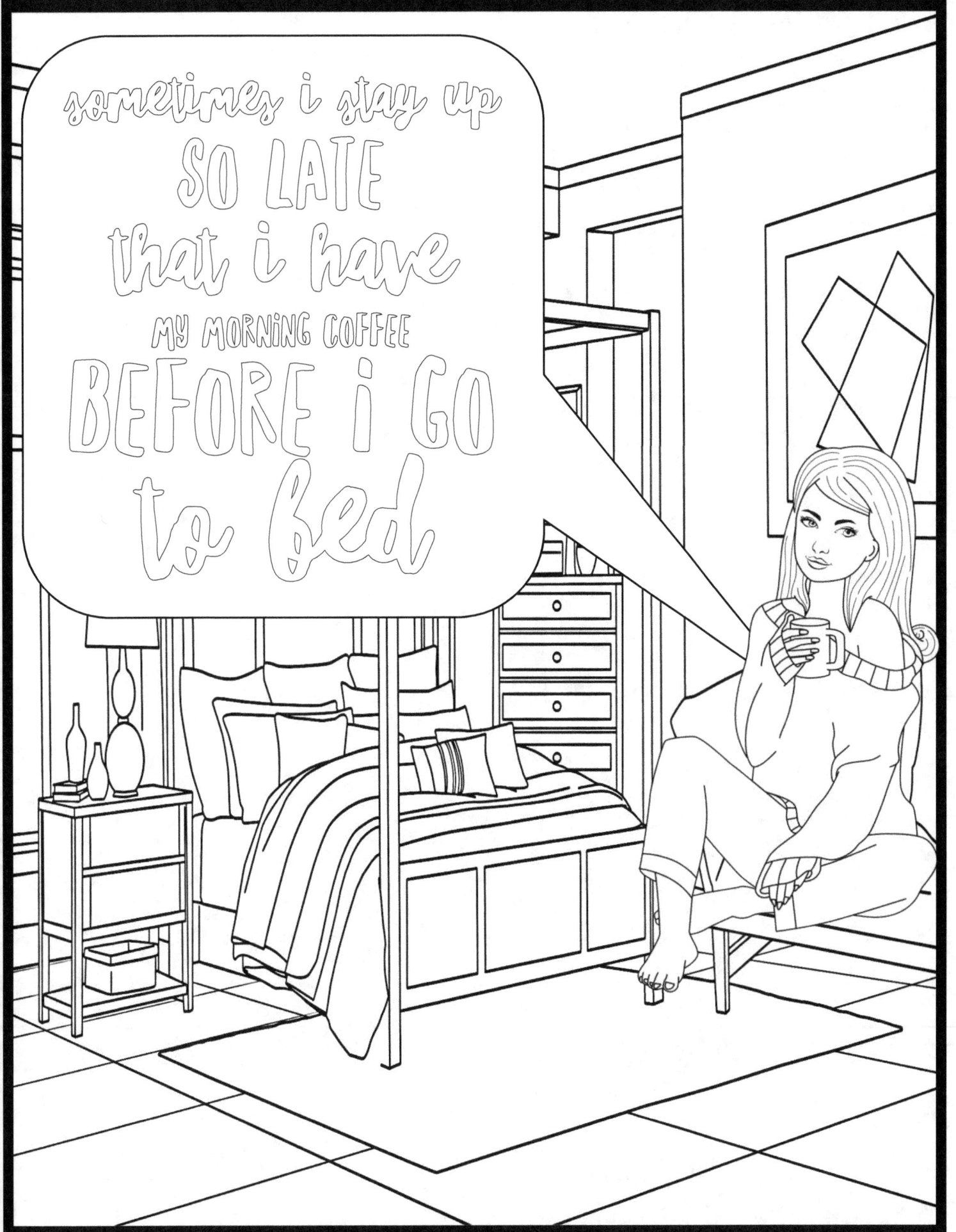

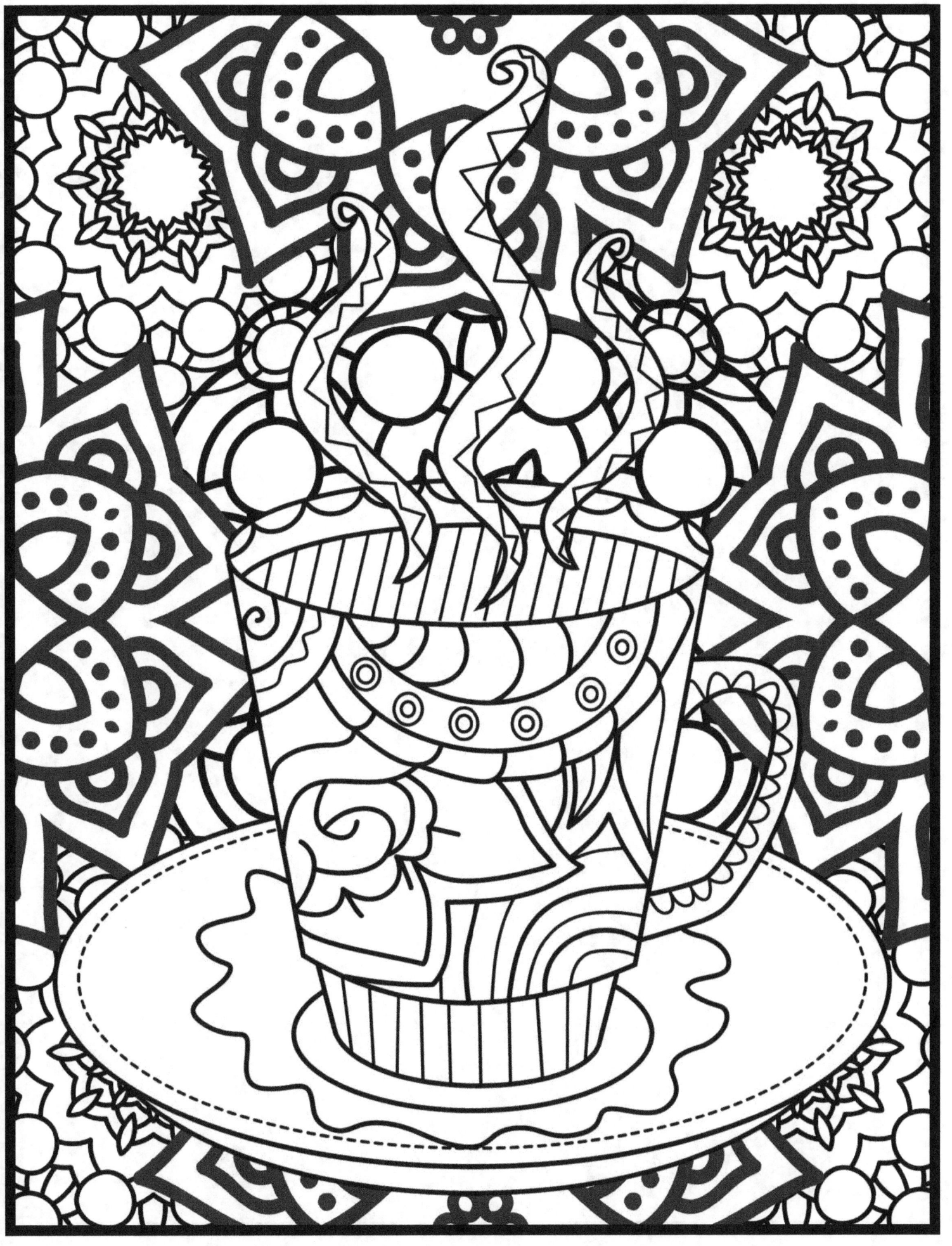

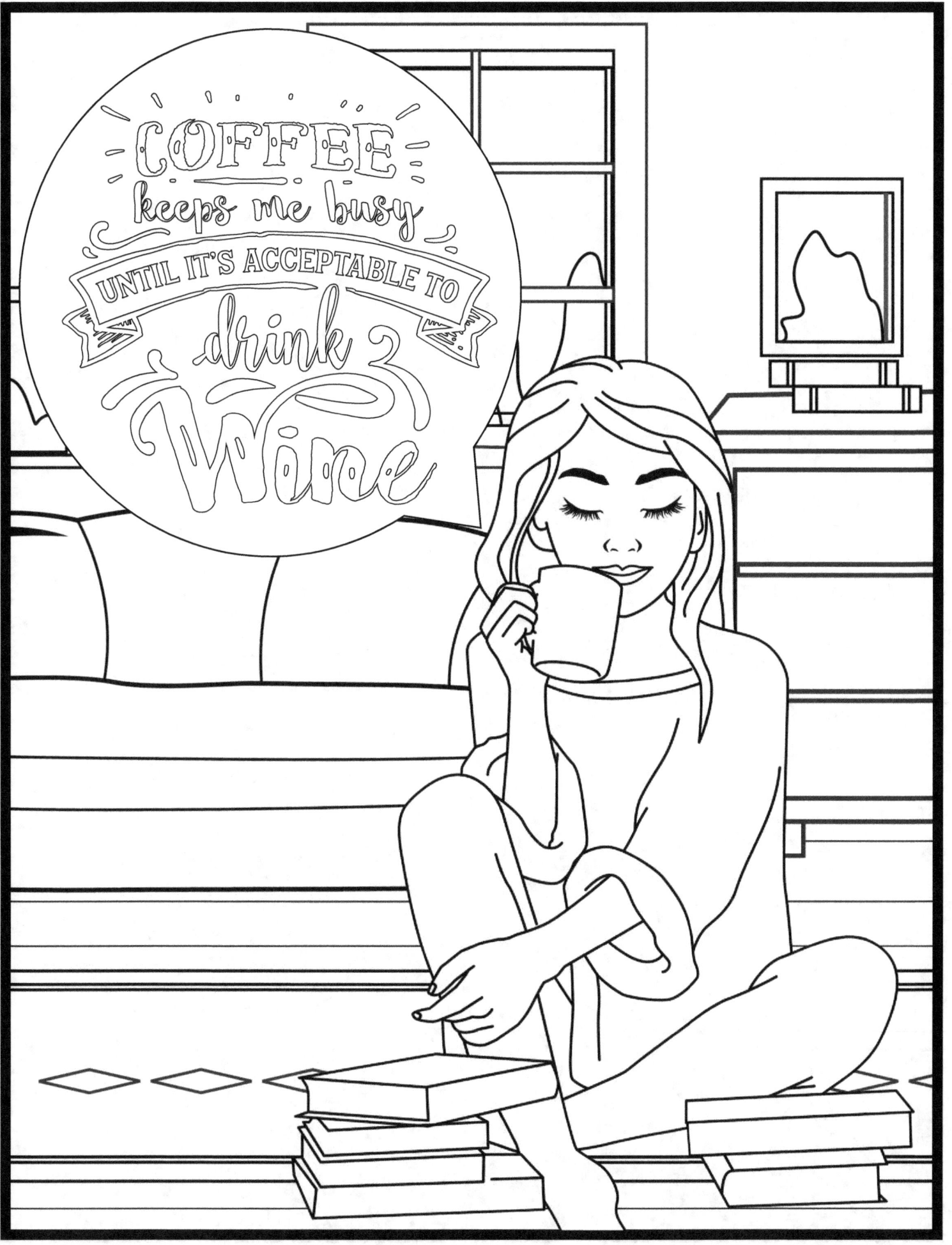

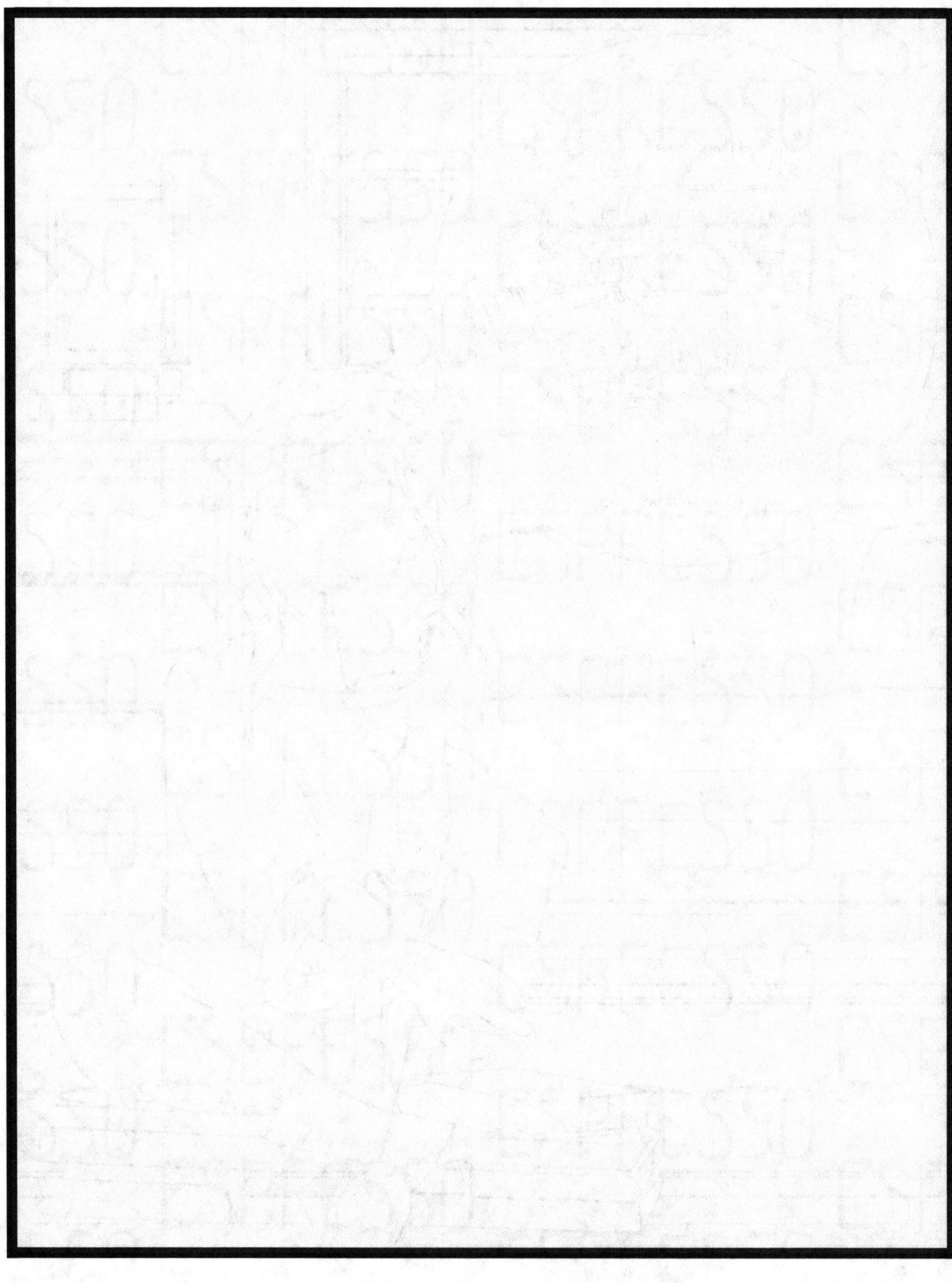

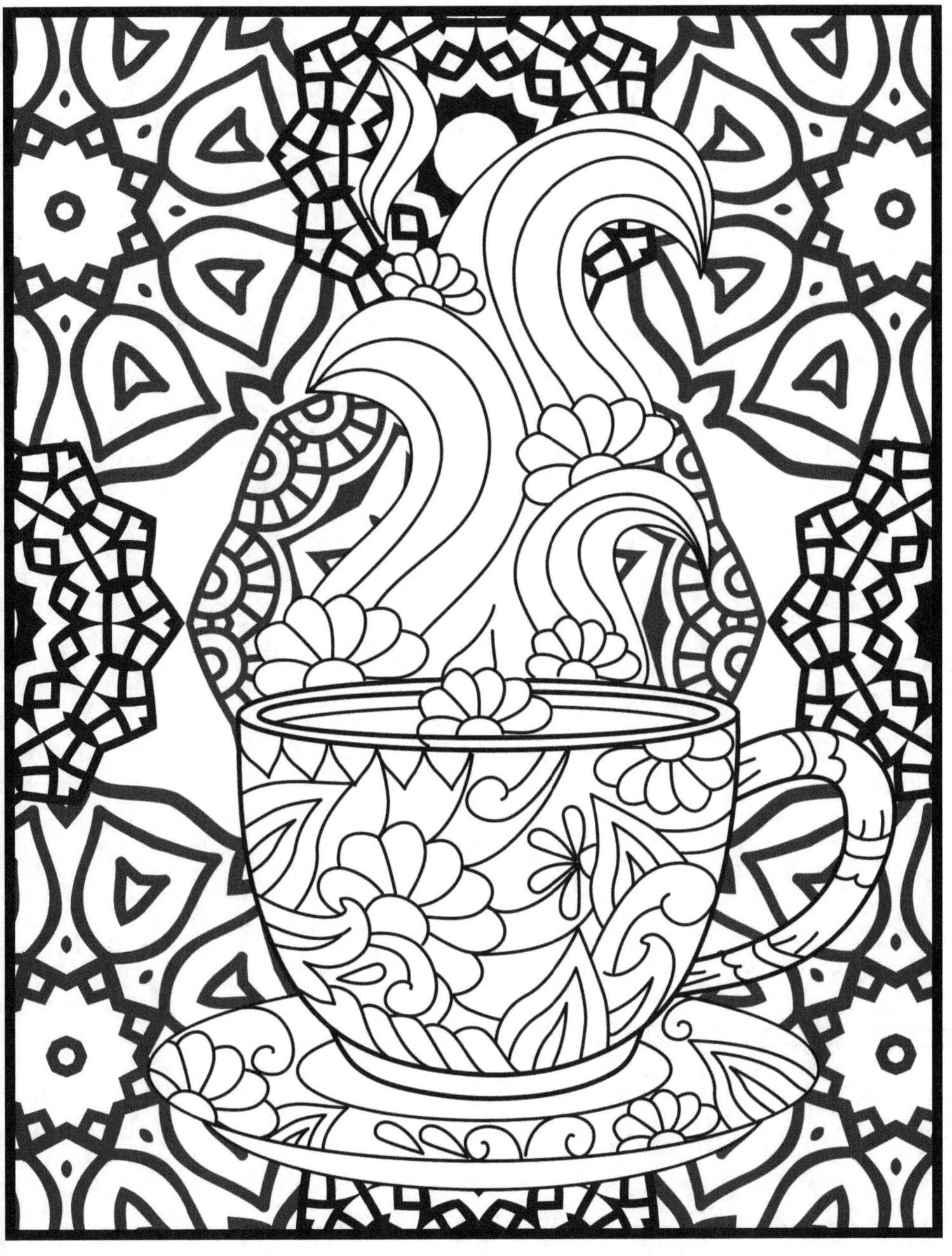

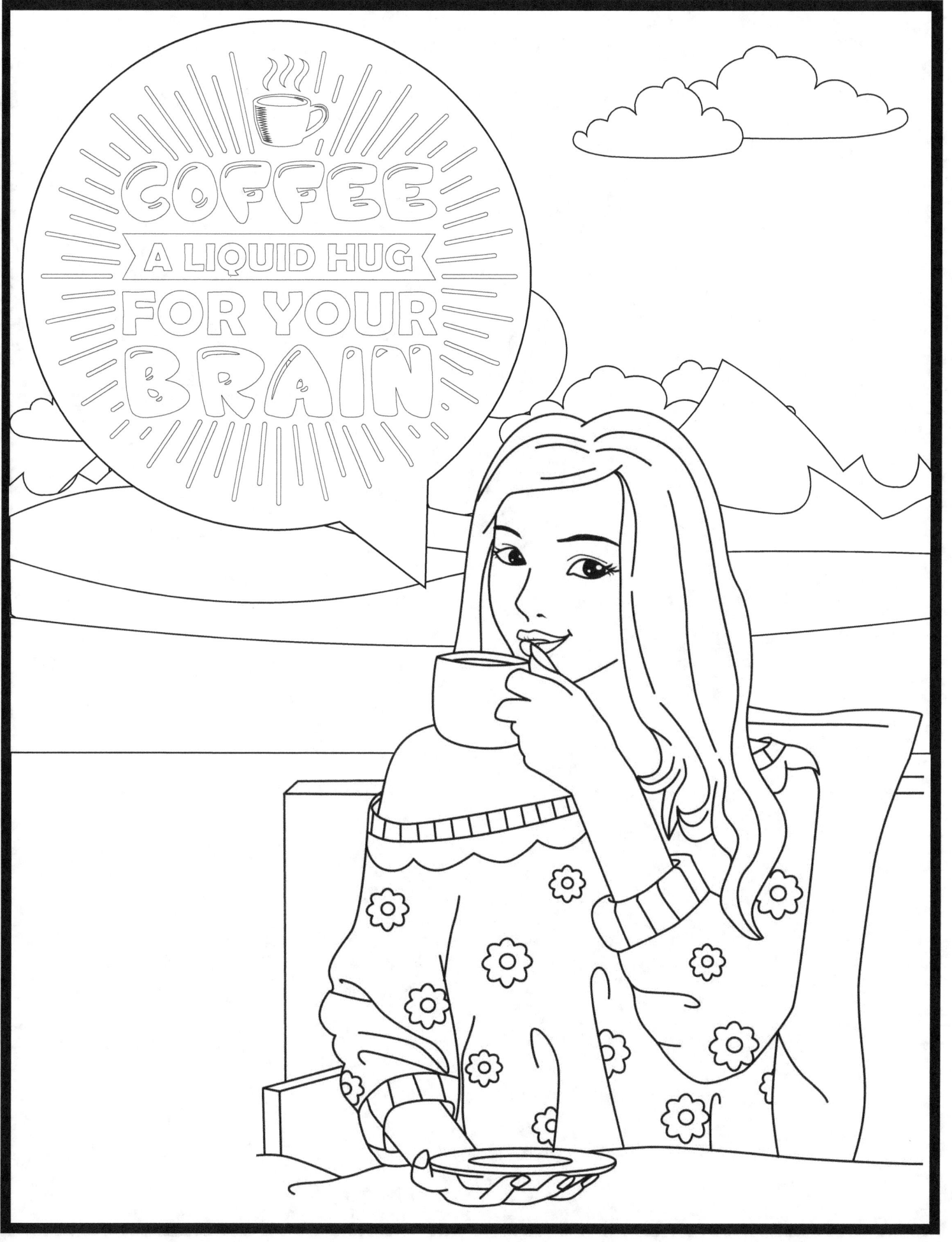

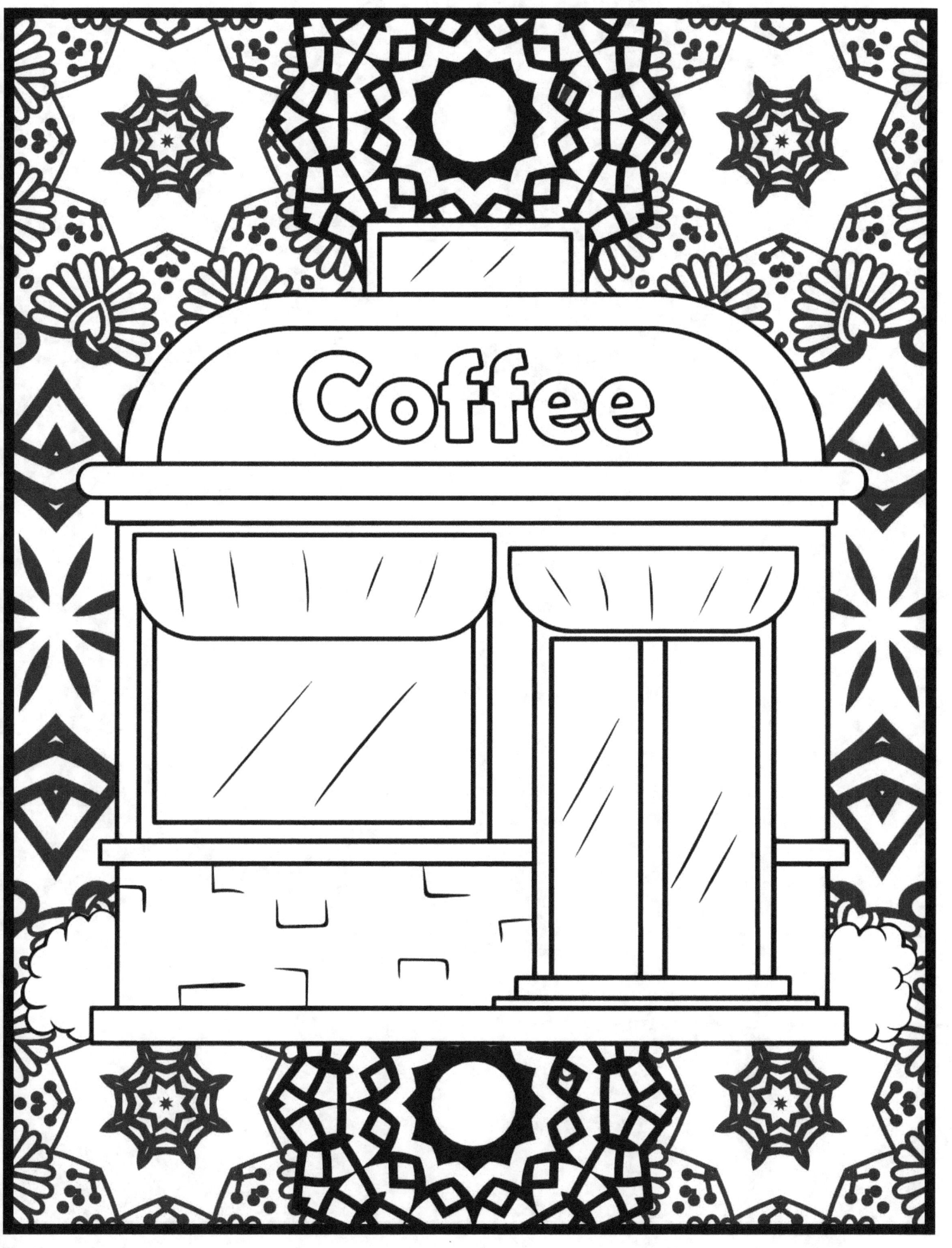

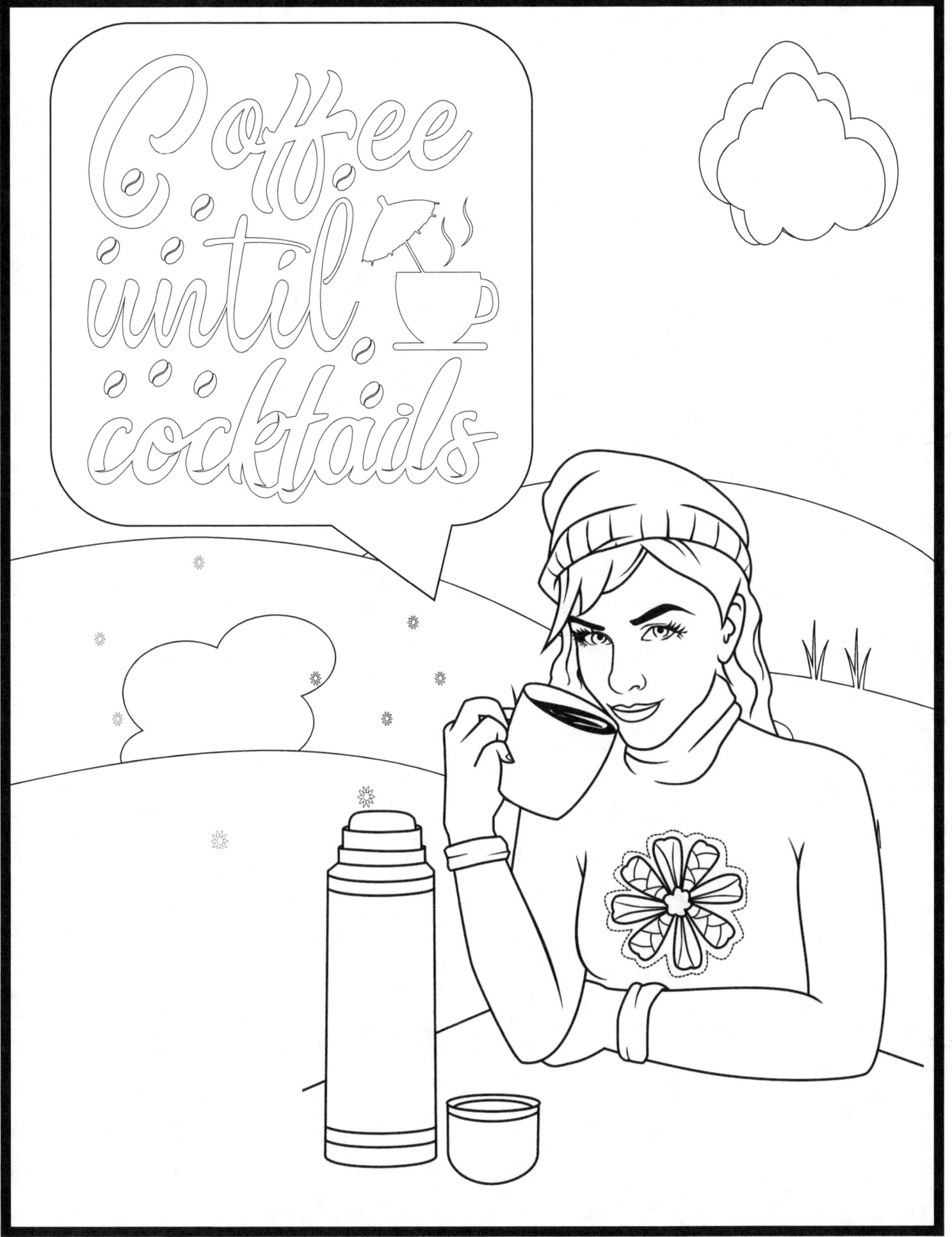

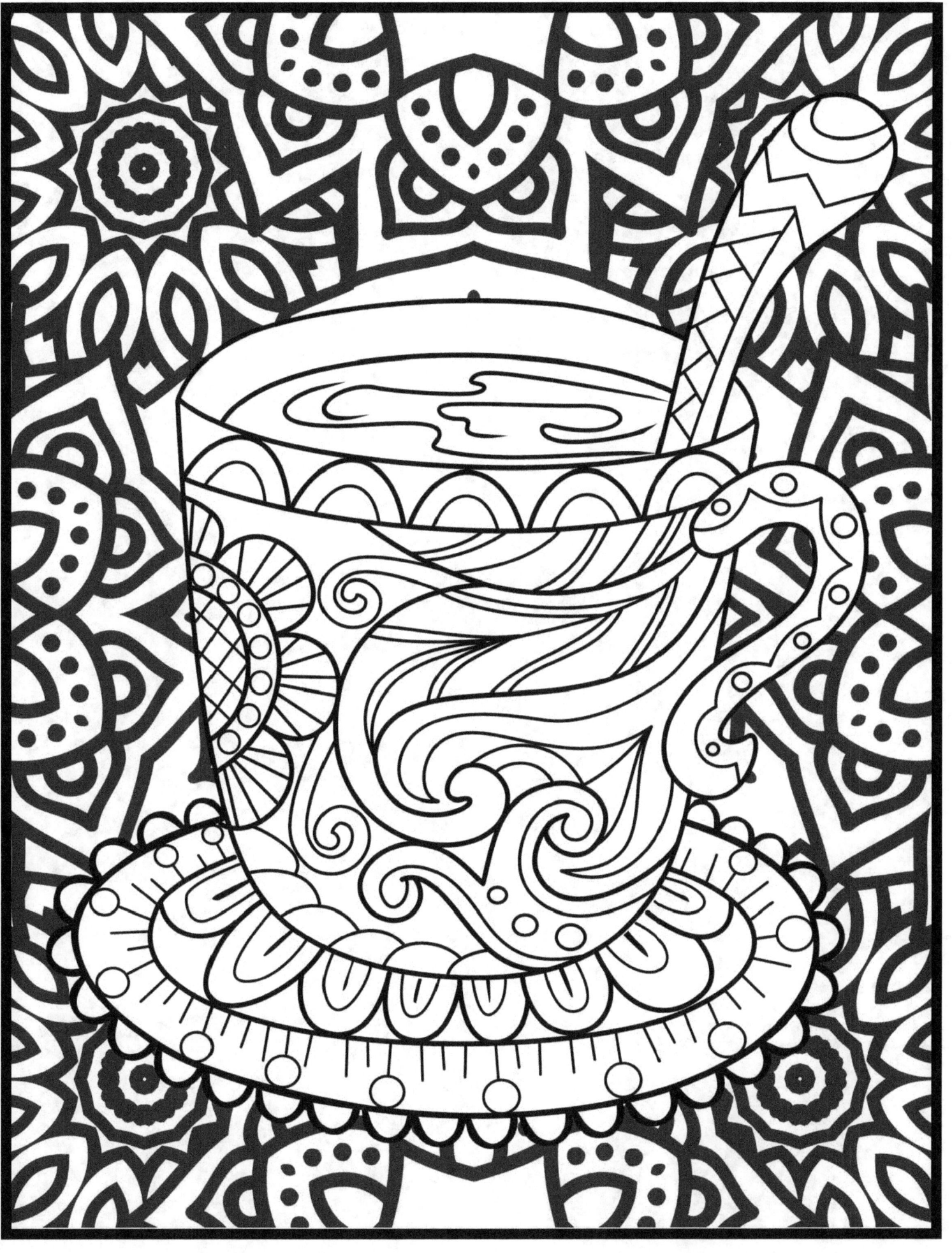

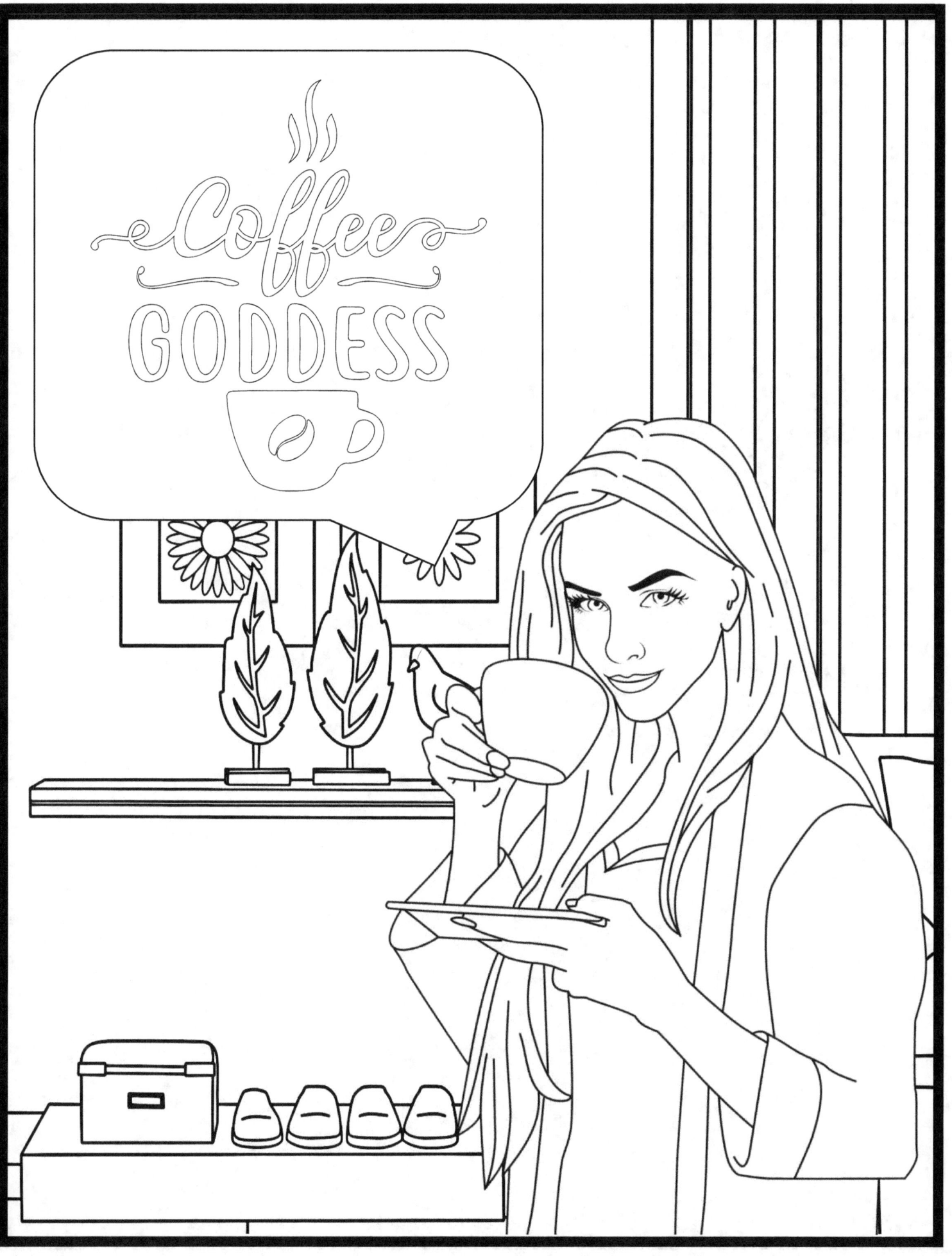

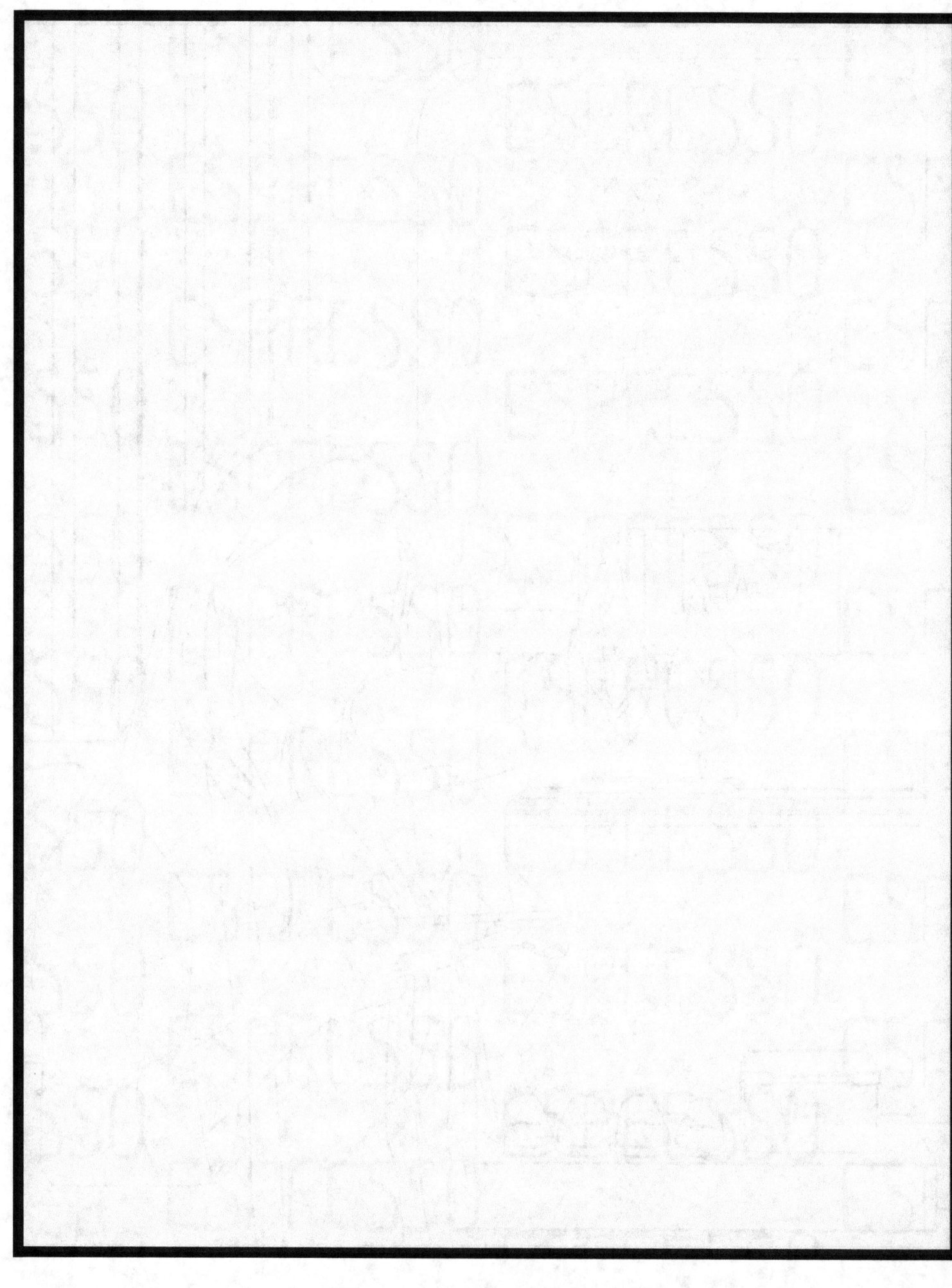

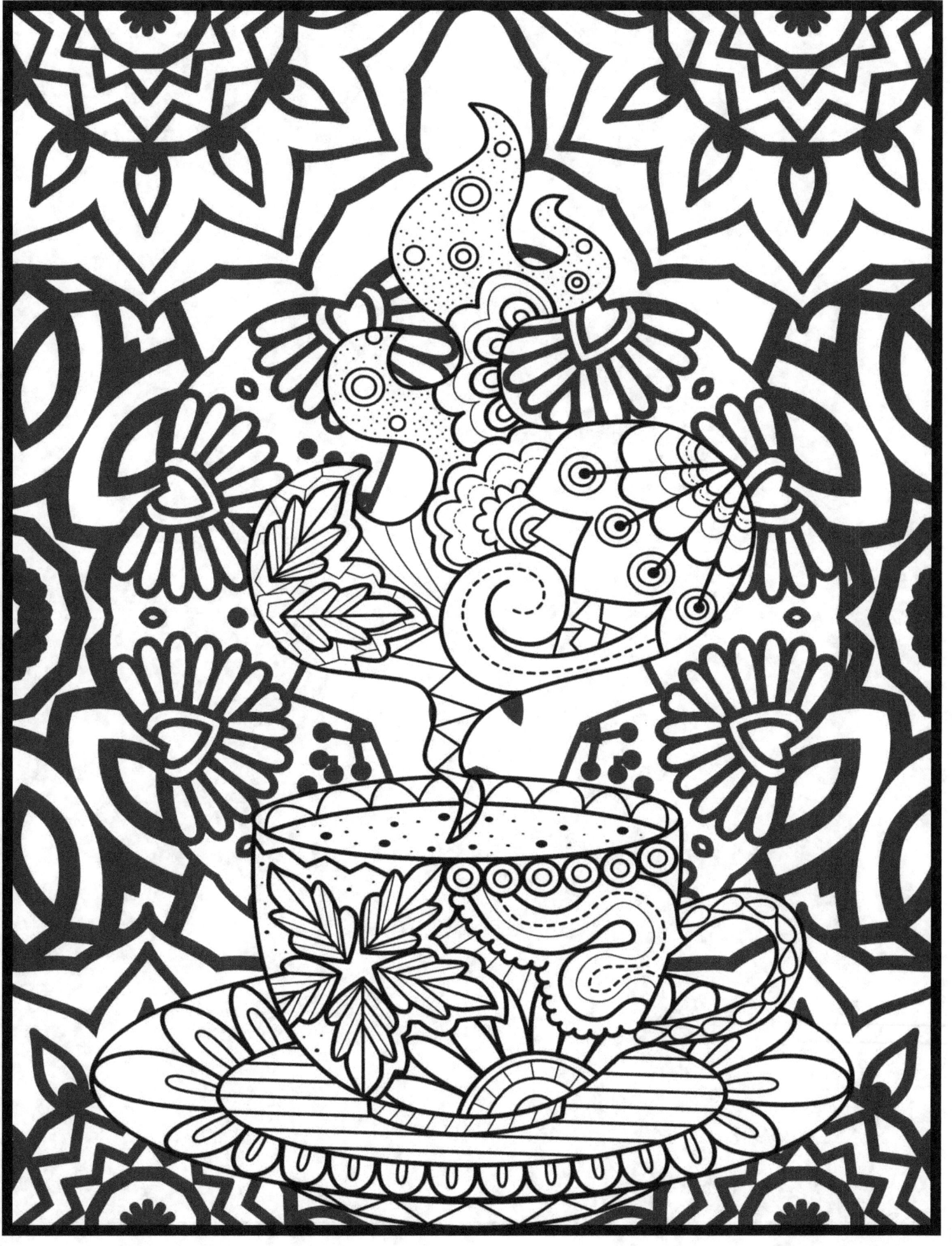

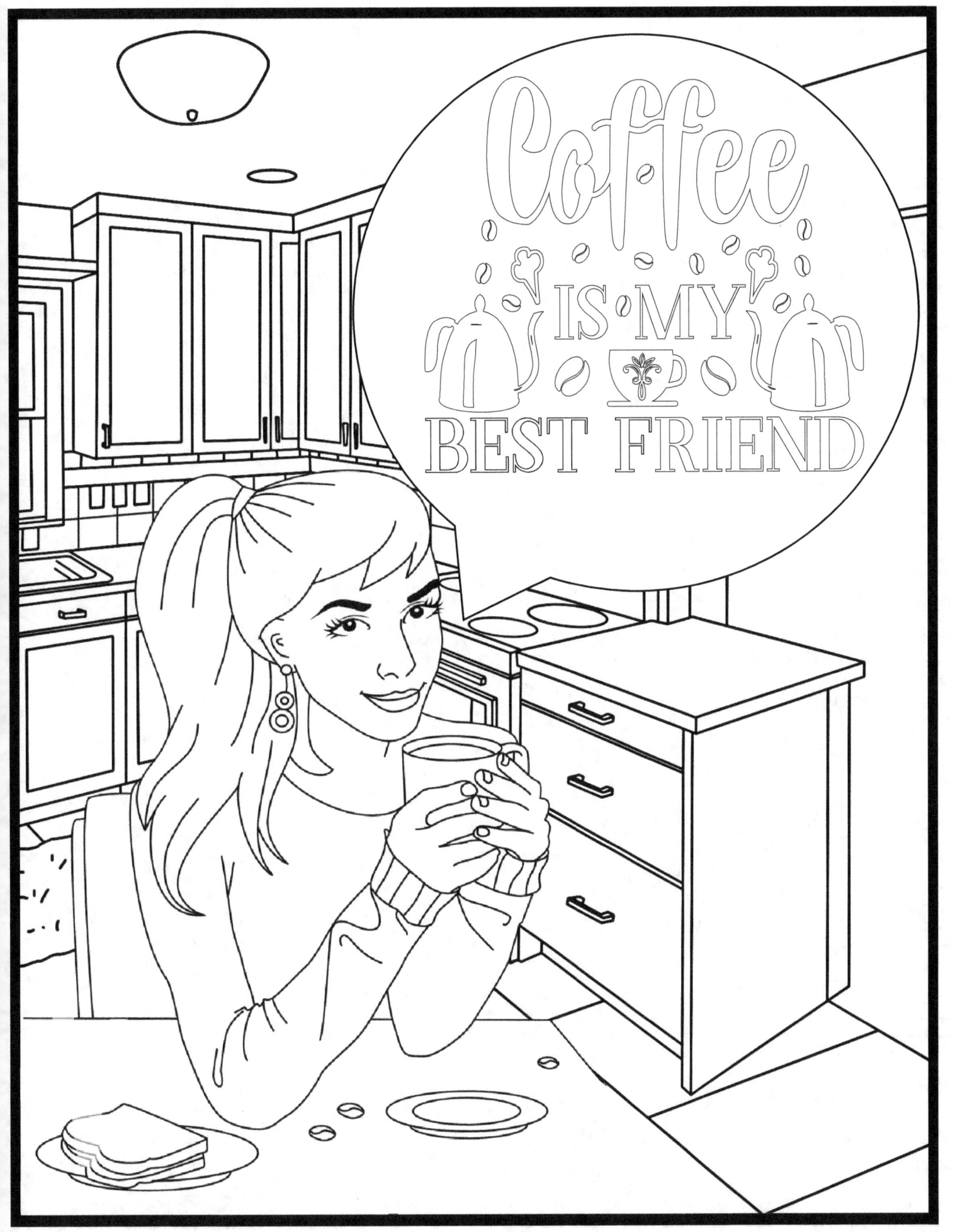

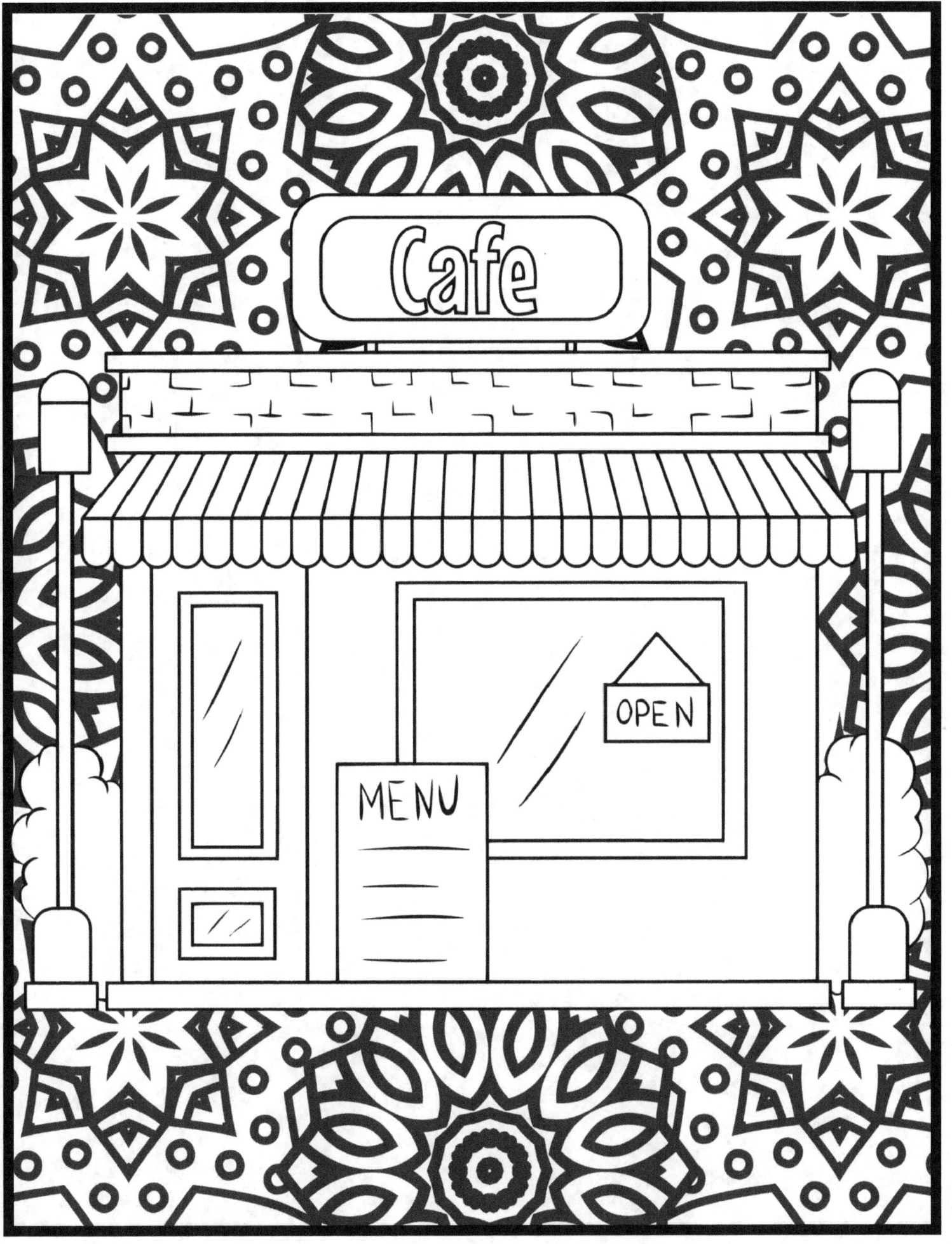

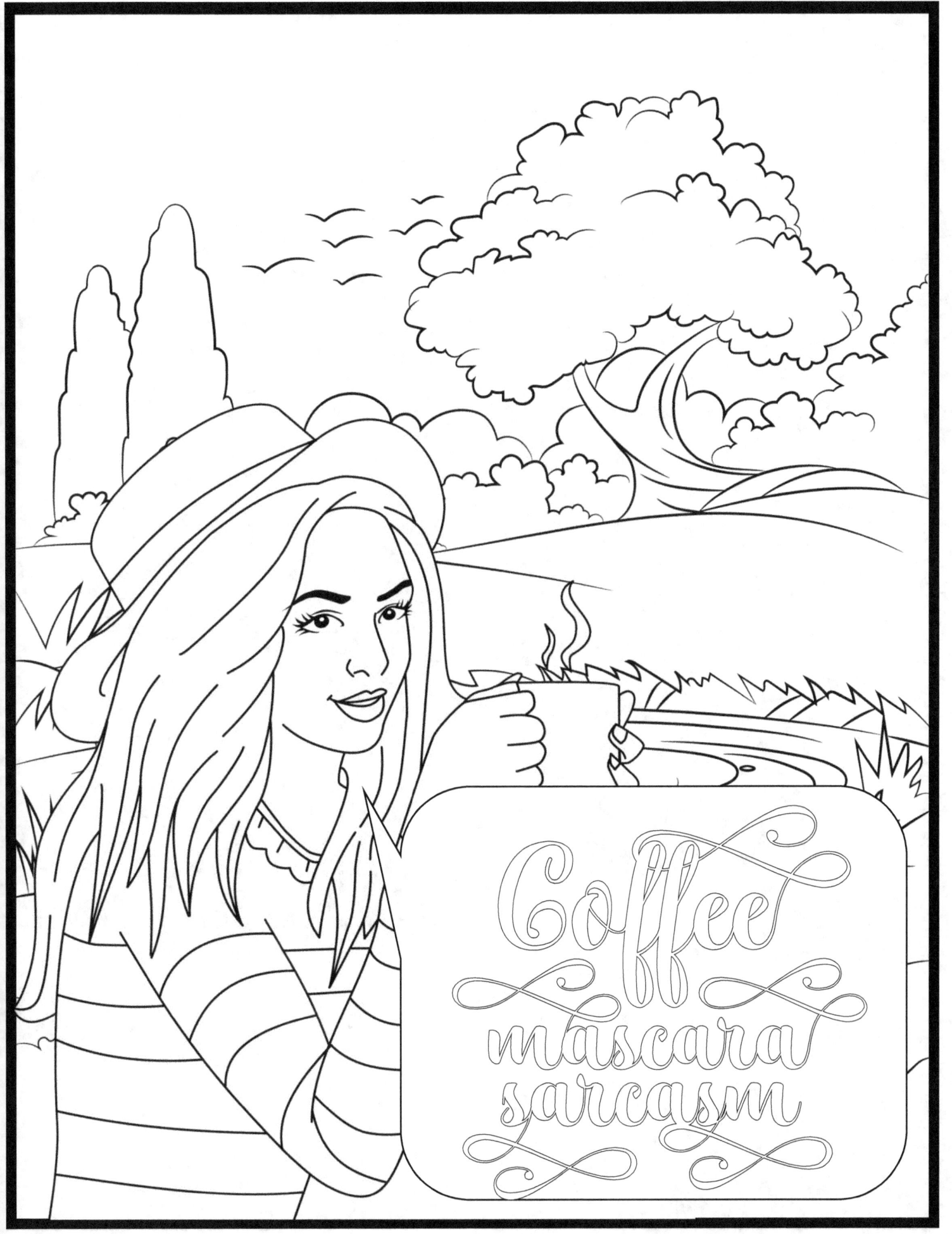

· CIAO ·

Thank you for your patronage!

TIME TO BUY ANOTHER BOOK!

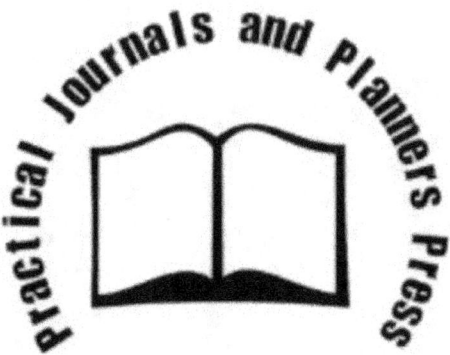

PRACTICALJOURNALSANDPLANNERS.COM

Copyright © 2020 Practical Journals and Planners
All rights reserved. No part of this book may be reproduced or transmitted in any form or by any means electronic or mechanical including photocopying, recording, scanning or any other information storage retrieval system without permission from the Publisher.

www.ingramcontent.com/pod-product-compliance
Lightning Source LLC
Chambersburg PA
CBHW080526220526
45465CB00006B/2611